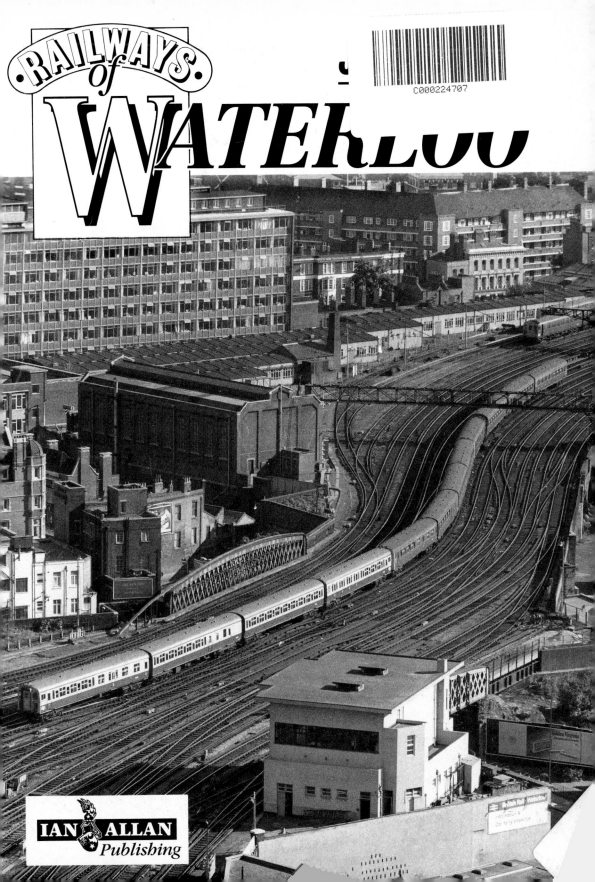

·RAILWAYS·
of
WATERLOO

C000224707

IAN ALLAN
Publishing

Previous page:
A view from the Shell tower on 7 September 1971.
J. H. Cooper-Smith

Right:
Waterloo seen from the air in mid-1993. The Victory Arch stands in front of the newly-completed International terminus, to the left much of the facade of the NSE station is obscured by scaffolding during the refurbishment of the old LSWR office blocks, from which the new footbridge emerges to cross Waterloo Road into the East station at the bottom left of the picture.
European Passenger Services

First published 1994

ISBN 0 7110 2237 2

© Ian Allan Ltd 1994

Designed by
Ian Allan Studio

Published by
Ian Allan Publishing
an imprint of Ian Allan
Ltd, Terminal House,
Station Approach,
Shepperton, Surrey
TW17 8AS; and printed
by Ian Allan Printing Ltd
Coombelands House,
Coombelands Lane,
Addlestone Weybridge
Surrey KT15 1HY.

Contents

	Preface	4
1	The LSWR Stations	5
2	The Southern Railway Era	25
3	The Postwar Years	37
4	The Coming of the International Station	47
5	Waterloo (East)	55
6	The Underworld	63
7	Trains and Traffic	69
	Select Bibliography	96

Preface

Front cover, top:
With the overall roof and
platform canopies of
Waterloo complementing
the scene, rebuilt 'Merchant
Navy' class 462 No 35014
Nederland Line blows off
noisily as the crew await
the right away in
September 1964. For many
years No 35014 was a Nine
Elms-based locomotive.
N. L. Browne

Front cover, bottom:
Old and new side by side at
Waterloo. A recently
introduced diesel multiple-
unit, No 159003, which
replaced diesel haulage on
the Exeter services during
1993, stands alongside a
more traditional electric
unit.
Brian Morrison

Back cover:
The curved approaches to
Waterloo can be seen in this
recent aerial view. The
International station is
beneath the overall roof on
the right, and the new
walkway between the two
Waterloo stations is the
tube-like structure in the
bottom left of the
photograph.

The publication of this book should coincide with Waterloo station becoming London's rail gateway to Europe. The elegant arch of Nicholas Grimshaw's International station and the massive steelwork of the roof of the Network SouthEast terminus are united by the sweeping curve of the dignified Edwardian-style buildings at the rear of the concourse. With many travellers perhaps seeing Waterloo for the first time, it is opportune to publish this brief introduction to the terminus, which will soon celebrate a century and a half of history.

I am indebted for much factual information to Alan Jackson, the expert on London's termini, and to R. A. Williams for his researches into LSWR history. Two railwaymen who worked at Waterloo, Reg Randell and Denis Cullum, provided memories and pictures. Facts and figures are gratefully acknowledged from the Public Affairs office of Network SouthEast's South Western Division, also from the National Railway Museum, the Public Record Office and the Railway Club library. Many photographers have contributed to illustrate this story, either directly or through the medium of the Ian Allan library.

J. N. Faulkner
Surbiton
August 1993

CHAPTER ONE

The LSWR Stations

T he London & Southampton Railway, in common with other pioneer main lines, commenced on the fringe of the capital's built-up area. Its terminus at Nine Elms, opened on 21 May 1838, was no further from the centre of affairs than Euston or Paddington but suffered from being on the other side of the Thames, whence a fourpenny steamer or a sixpenny omnibus was needed to reach the City.

The Richmond Railway had been promoted as a local line to a West End terminus on the South Bank near to Hungerford Bridge. The London & South Western Railway in agreeing to work the Richmond line, took over its powers and obtained an Act on 31 July 1845 for a Metropolitan Extension to a 10-acre site near the foot of Waterloo Bridge. A second Act on 2 July 1847 authorised the widening of the extension to accommodate four tracks and for additional land at the Waterloo Bridge terminus.

The two-mile route branched off the original line into Nine Elms and was carried throughout on embankment and a 235-arch viaduct, involving the demolition of about 700 houses. However, the line made a sweeping curve around the Vauxhall pleasure gardens, where an intermediate station was provided, like Nine Elms to the design of Sir William Tite. After overcoming some problems with the inspecting officer regarding the skew crossing over Westminster Bridge Road, the Waterloo Bridge station came into use on 11 July 1848 and Nine Elms closed to passenger traffic. The new terminus was usually known as Waterloo Bridge until 1882.

By an Act of 26 August 1846 the LSWR had obtained powers to extend its line to London Bridge and so reach the edge of the City. Some land was acquired, but the post-Mania financial collapse caused the abandonment of this costly scheme in 1849. The possibility that Waterloo Bridge might become only an intermediate station delayed the erection of permanent buildings until 1853, when the principal offices and passenger facilities were built alongside the main departure platform (No 1), a decision which was to cause much inconvenience in later years. Under its low wooden roof the station had four platforms and six tracks; the frontage faced a cab yard and a roadway which came up through a tunnel from Griffin Street, off York Road, and descended by another ramp into Waterloo Road. A similar roadway was provided for the arrival platforms. On the north side of the station a loco siding and turntable followed the course of the originally intended line towards Hungerford Bridge. The site of the 1848 station was in the area of today's platforms Nos 7 to 12.

With commendable foresight quadruple track had been provided on the approach viaduct to Waterloo. In 1845 there had been the possibility that the London & Brighton Railway and, during the mid-1850s, that the West End of London & Crystal Palace Railway would share the terminus. However, the northern pair of tracks came to be used by trains to and from the Windsor lines, as the Richmond Railway was known after its post-1848 extensions. It was traffic from this direction which required the first enlargement of the terminus on 3 August 1860. Three new platforms (Nos 5, 6 and 7) and four extra tracks were added to the north of the original station, which was then reserved for main line traffic.

In 1859 the South Eastern Railway promoted the Charing Cross Railway and sought to attract the LSWR into building a connection towards Charing Cross, but financial terms for running powers or for a contribution to the cost of Cannon Street station could not be agreed. Instead, in January 1864, the SER built a single-line connection from its Charing Cross route, crossing Waterloo Road and the concourse of the LSWR terminus, to join the siding between platforms Nos 2 and 3. A service of LNWR trains to London Bridge and latterly to Cannon Street used this link between 6 July 1865 and 1 January 1868, calling at a platform on the bridge known as New Waterloo to change the LSWR engine for a SER one. Finding this service unremunerative, the SER opened its Waterloo Junction station on 1 January 1869 and South Western commuters could walk across the footbridge alongside the connecting line and take a South Eastern train to Charing Cross or Cannon Street.

In the main terminus the Windsor line had been given its own booking office and waiting rooms opposite the three new platforms, while the main parcel office was also situated on this side of the station. In 1875 another cab roadway down to York Road was constructed in front of these buildings. The points and signals at the approach to the terminus came in 1867 under the control of the first 'A' box with 47 levers. This was successively enlarged and rebuilt in 1874, 1878, 1880 and 1885 before being replaced by a new 'A' box in 1892.

Sir William Tite's terminus building at Nine Elms survived for over a century after Waterloo replaced it in 1848. Seen here in Southern Railway days it was demolished after World War 2 and its site incorporated in the new Covent Garden flower market. Lens of Sutton

The growth in suburban traffic led to the opening on 16 December 1878 of the South station, intended to relieve the 1848 station of local trains to Epsom, Kingston and Hampton Court. Known as 'Cyprus', following the annexation of that colony, the South station consisted of a long wooden island platform (not numbered) under its own overall roof and with a separate concourse, booking office and refreshment room overlooking Waterloo Road. Between the South station and platform No 1 was a small loco shed and yard.

The next extension to the terminus was on the north side where the six roads of the North (or Windsor) line station came into use in stages during 1885; this being the year of the Sudan campaign it was dubbed 'Khartoum'. Its platforms were numbered 7 (backing on to the 1860 extension), 8, 9 and 10, usually known as the 'Milk'. The others handled the Windsor line local services, allowing the 1860 Windsor line platforms to be used for main line arrivals. The North station was covered by a substantial iron roof and behind the concourse were more offices, which continued alongside the roadway down to York Road in a separate block which housed the company's management. From 1886 the three sections of the terminus were termed officially as South, Central and North.

There was also another and unique station at Waterloo. In 1854 the London Necropolis Co had established its large cemetery at Brookwood, to which it ran funeral trains from a platform on the south side of the line adjacent to Westminster Bridge Road. In order to make room for the tracks into the 1878 South station, one line and the outer wall of the Necropolis station had been removed, but the company had been granted extended tenure over the remainder.

An artist's sketch of Waterloo station at the time of opening in July 1848, showing one of the vehicular ramps from Westminster Bridge Road and some of the temporary buildings.
Courtesy of the National Railway Museum

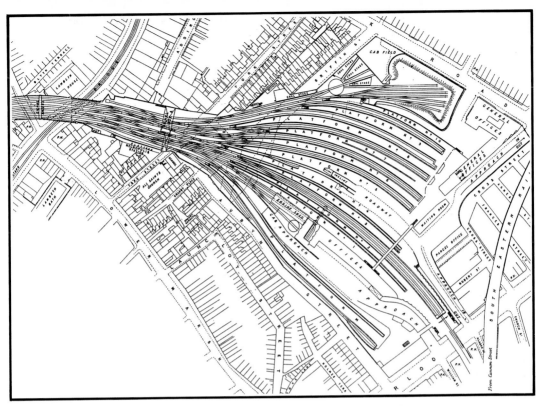

Waterloo station in the mid-1890s. After 1898 the area between Aubyn Street, Launcelot Street and Holmes Terrace was occupied by the Waterloo & City power station and sidings. All Saints Church and School were the most notable of the buildings in the 6½ acres of property acquired for the site of the new South station.

In 1891 the viaduct between Vauxhall and Waterloo was widened for two extra tracks; a second up line on the main line side and another down Windsor line. As part of these improvements a new 'A' box was installed in May 1892 with 220 levers controlling 247 semaphore signals, many of them mounted above the box as route indicators. A system of gearing enabled the 220 levers to do the work of 350. There was also the 'Crows Nest' cabin up in the roof of the Central station and a small box controlling the North sidings.

Waterloo had grown piecemeal into a confusing and inefficient station. Divided into three distinct sections, its 18 tracks shared only 10 platform numbers. The long platforms Nos 2 and 3 extended almost to the screen wall above Waterloo Road and, with the connecting line to the SER, formed a barrier to movement along the concourse. A small drawbridge spanned the through line and a footbridge opposite the booking office on platform No 1 provided a short cut to platform No 3 and beyond. Platforms Nos 2 and 3, which handled some of the principal services, were narrow and the double-sided tracks between platforms Nos 1 and 2 and between Nos 3 and 4 added to the confusion. By the turn of the century Waterloo was beyond a joke and the LSWR had become the subject of press criticism. Moreover, the terminus was no longer adequate for the growing traffic.

Above:
A driver's view of Waterloo from the footplate of an engine running tender first on the up Windsor line about 1870. The screen wall of the original Necropolis station is on the right, the 1848 platforms are straight ahead and the 1860 Windsor extension to the left. Above the line stands the first 'A' box erected in 1867. British Rail

Right:
The April 1867 working timetable explained to drivers the meaning of the newly-installed signals seen in the previous picture on the gantry alongside 'A' box. Author's collection

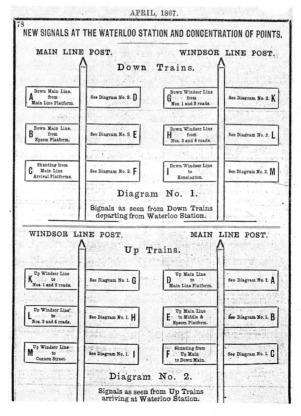

APRIL, 1867.

78

NEW SIGNALS AT THE WATERLOO STATION AND CONCENTRATION OF POINTS.

MAIN LINE POST.   **WINDSOR LINE POST.**

Down Trains.

A	Down Main Line. from Main Line Platform.	See Diagram No. 2. D	G	Down Windsor Line from Nos. 1 and 2 roads.	See Diagram No. 2. K
B	Down Main Line. from Epsom Platform.	See Diagram No. 2. E	H	Down Windsor Line from Nos. 3 and 4 roads.	See Diagram No. 2. L
C	Shunting from Main Line Arrival Platforms.	See Diagram No. 2. F	I	Down Windsor Line to Kensington.	See Diagram No. 2. M

Diagram No. 1.

Signals as seen from Down Trains departing from Waterloo Station.

WINDSOR LINE POST.   **MAIN LINE POST.**

Up Trains.

K	Up Windsor Line to Nos. 1 and 2 roads.	See Diagram No. 1. G	D	Up Main Line to Main Line Platform.	See Diagram No. 1. A
L	Up Windsor Line to Nos. 3 and 4 roads.	See Diagram No. 1. H	E	Up Main Line to Middle & Epsom Platform.	See Diagram No. 1. B
M	Up Windsor Line to Cannon Street.	See Diagram No. 1. I	F	Shunting from Up Main to Down Main.	See Diagram No. 1. C

Diagram No. 2.

Signals as seen from Up Trains arriving at Waterloo Station.

Right:
The 1878 extension South station's platforms and concourse seen from Waterloo Road. The classical facade on the right belongs to the Central station, with the bridge to the SECR at Waterloo Junction emerging from its arches. The signs of demolition to the left of the picture may indicate that it was taken at the start of the rebuilding in 1902.
Courtesy of the National Railway Museum

Centre right:
The two-platform South station had its own concourse with booking office, bookstall and florist's shop etc. British Rail

Bottom right:
A commercial postcard view dating from the turn of the century showing the principal buildings alongside the double-sided platform No 1, the footbridge to platform No 3 and beyond and passengers alighting from a main line train which has arrived at platform No 2.
Lens of Sutton

12 *Right:*
*The through line to the
SECR crossed the middle of
the Central station
concourse, but when not in
use a drawbridge provided
a level passageway for
barrows. Prominent signs
direct the traveller to the
two other sections of the
terminus and the arrival
indicator can be glimpsed
on platform No 2.
Drummond 'M7' tanks
stand at the rear of trains in
platforms Nos 2 and 3; the
one on the right is standing
on the stub end of road No
6 which remained after
platform No 3 was widened
in 1902.*
Courtesy of the National
Railway Museum

Below right:
*An animated scene
alongside the incoming cab
roadway following the
arrival of an important
train (perhaps from
Southampton Docks)
behind an Adams 4-4-0 on
platform No 5. Hansom
cabs and an inter-station
omnibus await passengers
and their stacks of luggage.
Among the smartly-dressed
crowd and the army of
porters are some of the
denizens of Waterloo,
hoping to earn an honest
penny by carrying bags or
holding horses' heads.*
Courtesy of the National
Railway Museum

Right:
Beyond the arrival roadway can be seen the platforms of the 1860 extension and the 1885 Windsor line North station, whose roof girders are visible behind the departure indicator. The Windsor line booking office is on the right and the directions to the City Railway entrance in the background indicate that this picture was taken after the Waterloo & City Railway opened in 1898. British Rail

Below:
From the outer end of platform No 1, 'T9' 4-4-0 No 120 (now part of the national collection) is seen waiting to leave with a train to Southampton, while in platform No 3, 'M7' 0-4-4T No 240 heads a train for Guildford via Woking. Ian Allan Library

Above:
A general view of the Central station platforms taken from the small loco yard between the South station and platform No 1. Class L11 4-4-0 No 408 stands in platform No 2 on a down main line stopping train.
Loco Publishing Co/IAL

Right:
Adams '460' class 4-4-0 No 476 waits at the end of the platforms. To the left can be seen the small North cabin which controlled the sidings and loco yard beyond the Windsor line station.
Loco Publishing Co/IAL

Below right:
Adams Radial 4-4-2T No 420 on the turntable in the old Windsor line loco yard. In the platforms of the North station is a 'block' train formed of four-wheel stock of 1873 vintage.
Loco Publishing Co/IAL

The site for any extension would have to be the area of squalid property beyond the existing South station. During 1898 the LSWR board considered plans for rebuilding and promoted a Bill for the necessary powers. This met with much local opposition and had to be withdrawn. Returning to Parliament in the 1899 session, the LSWR first placated its critics by contributing to road improvement, by building a series of tenement blocks to house the 1,750 displaced inhabitants, by moving the church school and granting an annuity to the vicar who had lost his parish. The Necropolis station was in a key position obstructing the enlargement. Consequently, the LSWR had to build the company a new station and office block on the south side of the line beyond Westminster Bridge Road, to renew their 999-year lease granted in 1878 and compensate them for disturbance. These obstacles removed, the LSWR Bill received Royal Assent on 9 August 1899.

The LSWR board gradually accepted the idea that the new extension should be built as part of a complete reconstruction of the station. Work started quickly on the new Necropolis station which came into use on 16 February 1902. Meanwhile the local residents had been rehoused and by early 1903 site clearance had been completed and the first contracts had been let for sub-structure work. During the early 1900s progress was slow; the company had many competing demands on its financial resources and in some years profits were poor. Steelwork for the lofty new roof, which would extend over the top of the old South station began to be erected in November 1905. Eventually, in January 1909 new platforms Nos 1 to 3 came into use and the old South station was then closed.

A start was made in 1909 in building new offices and public amenities behind the new concourse and a spacious booking hall was opened here on 11 June 1911. Platforms Nos 4 and 5 on the site of the old South station had already come into use and December 1911 saw the completion of inclined roadways from Lower Marsh and Westminster Bridge Road, replacing the old evil-smelling tunnels. The bridge across Westminster Bridge Road had been widened between 1906 and 1908 to provide 11 tracks on the immediate approach to the station. This formed part of the LSWR's aim to have eight running lines between Waterloo and Clapham Junction, which was achieved by 1918, except for the section through Queens Road Battersea station. The former loco yard between the South and Central stations was replaced by enlargement of the yard in the South sidings near the Necropolis station, while the Windsor line yard and turntable were resited nearer to York Road.

Reconstruction was now reaching the heart of the old station. The advent of Hugh Drummond as LSWR chairman in 1911 and of Herbert Walker as general manager in 1912 brought a fresh impetus and decision to the project. The board now authorised progress to go forward steadily in planned stages. An important change from the original design was the retention of the 1885 Windsor line station; the structure was in good condition and, though two of the planned 23 platforms would be lost, this could be offset by the decline in inner suburban traffic and the prospect of electrification. Considerable cost would be avoided.

Use of the through connection to the South Eastern had decreased following the SER/LCDR merger and powers were obtained in 1911 for its abandonment, which took place on 26 March 1911. By now the new steelwork was taking shape among and above the buildings of the 1848 Central station and various temporary passageways and roofs were erected – users of Euston during the 1960s will be able to visualise the scene. Most of the old offices along platform No 1 had gone by 1913 and new wide stairways linked the concourse to Waterloo Road and the Waterloo & City line. By April 1913 the new roof was complete as far as platform No 11 and the opening of the Surrey Dining Room and the concourse's circular buffet on 27 June was marked by a luncheon for the LSWR's guests.

The next stage was the reconstruction and lengthening of the old arrival platforms to become the new platforms Nos 12-15. First the Windsor line platforms Nos 16-21 required realignment and rebuilding in concrete to make them ready for the electric trains expected in 1915. Beyond the central archway opposite platforms Nos 11 and 12, the office block would continue to the far end of the Windsor line concourse with, at platform level, a suburban booking office and more waiting rooms and

This map shows the situation in mid-1910. All five platforms of the new South station are completed, but the new office block behind the concourse and the approach roads from Lower Marsh and Westminster Bridge Road are not yet in use. The widening over Westminster Bridge Road is finished in readiness for the rebuilding of the former Central and North stations. The engine spurs outside platforms Nos 1-4 were removed after electrification. The roofing over the W&C sidings is apparent in this plan.

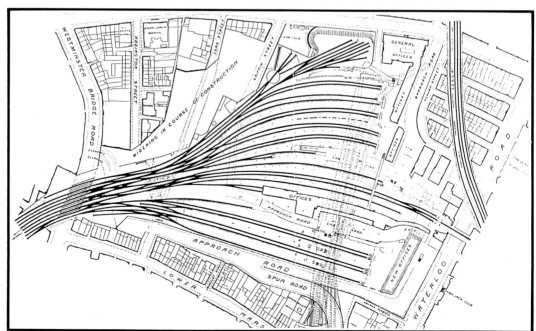

refreshment facilities. Behind these buildings a wide roadway led down to York Road, forming a continuous circuit from the access roads on the south side of the station. Another roadway from Griffin Street emerged from a tunnel into the central cab road between platforms Nos 11 and 12.

Although early completion of the rebuilding had been planned, the outbreak of World War 1 interrupted work on the new office buildings. Progress continued on the reconstruction of the arrival platforms Nos 12-15 which were needed to handle Waterloo's heavy wartime traffic and all came into use during 1916/17. Similarly the Windsor line platforms (Nos 16-21) were ready and equipped for the first electric trains on 25 October 1915. Electric services from the main line platforms Nos 1-6 commenced on 30 January 1916. An escalator from the concourse to the Waterloo & City line had been ordered from the USA in 1914 and this was eventually installed in April 1919.

With the return of peace, the completion of the new station could be resumed. The overall roof above the concourse was continued beyond platform No 11 and linked to the existing structure over the Windsor line platforms. Behind the suburban booking office was a large and ornate buffet and nearby was the genteel Windsor tea room, both opened during 1921. The retention of the 1885 North station had left a space vacant between platforms Nos 15 and 16; here a staff block, including the stationmaster's office, was built in 1919 and came to be known as the 'Village'. As a final embellishment to the new station the flamboyant Victory Arch was erected at the head of the flight of steps from the Windsor line concourse to the York

The original plan of reconstruction was for this terminus with 23 platforms, with 10 of them allocated to Windsor line traffic. The north end of the Windsor side concourse would have been narrower and the principal main line platforms shorter than in the revised 21 platform version. This plan shows the situation of the Necropolis station on its new site.

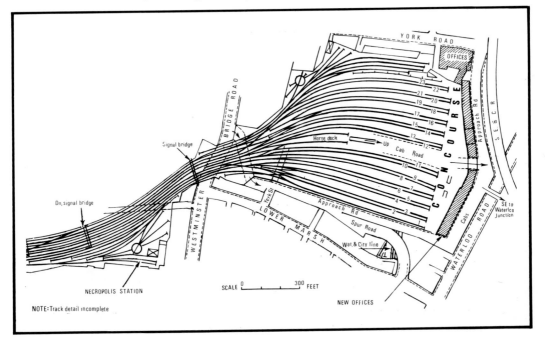

NECROPOLIS STATION

NOTE: Track detail incomplete

SCALE 0 — 300 FEET

NEW OFFICES

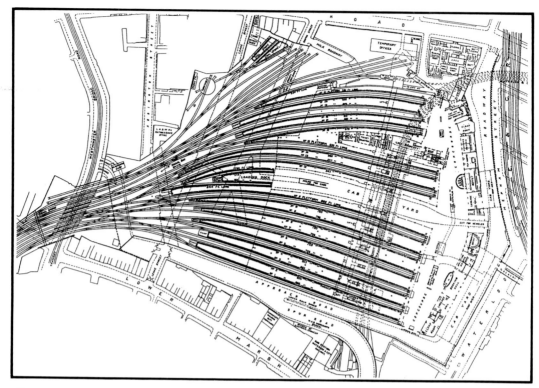

Above:
This detailed plan shows the reconstructed station as completed in 1922. The 'exit and entrance for foot passengers' is in fact the Victory arch and beside it is the main entrance from the concourse to the LSWR general offices on the corner of York Road. Below platform level can be seen the passenger and luggage subways and the Waterloo & City tracks.

Right:
Work on the sub-structure of the new South station extension is almost complete, together with the side wall and the approach from Westminster Bridge Road. This picture probably dates from mid-1905.
British Rail

Road approach. This was to form the memorial to the 585 LSWR staff who had lost their lives in World War 1 and it was here that Queen Mary (in the absence of King George V) officially opened the new station on 21 March 1922. The station itself stands as a memorial to engineers E. Andrews, J. W. Jacomb-Hood and A. W. Szlumper, also to architect J. R. Scott. The complete project, occupying more than two decades, had cost a total of £2,269,354. A chronology of the complicated transformation follows.

| Old station | | | | | New station | |
Platform	Road	Renumbered (1/10/12)	(7/12/13)	Out of Use	Platform	Into Use
New Extension					1	24/01/09
					2	24/01/09
					3	24/01/09
South station						
– {	1			24/01/09	4	25/07/09
{	2			24/01/09	5	06/03/10
Central station						
Cab Road & approach					5A/6	09/03/13
Station Offices					6/7	29/06/13
					6A/8	20/07/13
1	3	6		29/06/13	9	21/12/13
2 {	3			03/07/11		
{	4				10	21/12/13
Middle Road	5			removed 1902		
3 {	6-5 from			3/07/11	11	07/12/13
{	7 1902	7		1/10/13		Cab roadway
4	7					Dock sidings 8/14
Dock	8	8	Siding	08/14		
5	9	9	12	25/04/15	12	20/08/16
6 {	10	10	13	25/04/15	13	27/08/16
{	11	11	14	25/04/15	14	29/10/16
7	12	12	15	25/04/15	15	30/05/17
North station						
7	13	13	16	Reconstructed	16	13/06/15
8 {	14	14	17	Reconstructed	17	11/04/15
{	15	15	18	Reconstructed	18	11/04/15
9 {	16	16	19	Reconstructed	19	14/06/14
{	17	17	20	Reconstructed	20	14/02/15
10	18	Milk	Milk	Reconstructed	21	28/02/15

New platforms 5A, 6 and 6A were renumbered 6, 7 and 8 respectively from 1 October 1913.

After being taken out of public use platform lines were sometimes retained as sidings, while new lines were formed and used as sidings during the construction of platforms.

Right:

The five platforms in the new South station were completed early in 1910 and a picture taken at that time shows a suburban train in platform No 2 and a 'T9' on a up Bournemouth restaurant car express in platform No 5. The columns supporting the roof of the new station rise through the canopy over the departure side cab roadway in front of the old Central station buildings alongside old platform No 1.
Loco Publishing Co/IAL

Centre right:

Another view of the new platforms in 1910, perhaps with the same restaurant car express in platform No 5, and unusually a local train in platform No 2 double headed by 'T1' 0-4-4T No 363 and a 'M7' tank. The office block behind the concourse is nearing completion and the subway from the platforms to the Waterloo & City line is open, but the luggage lifts are not yet in service.
Loco Publishing Co/IAL.

Bottom right:

The first stage of the buildings behind the new platforms is structurally complete with a further section in progress. However, a piece of the old South station roof still projects beyond the new building on to the site of the cab roadway which will eventually encircle the front of the new station. The new booking hall here was not opened until June 1911.
Courtesy of the National Railway Museum.

Above:
A view of the concourse in 1913. The steelwork for the new roof now extends across the site of the old Central station, but a fragment of the original roof remains below it. Platform numbering beyond No 5 is still temporary.
Commercial postcard — Author's collection.

Right:
The scene in 1915 during the reconstruction of the 1860 part of the terminus. On the right is the screen wall of the 1885 North station with the old platform No 7 in front and the columns for the new roof being erected. The columns in the foreground mark the line of the new platform No 15 and the area between became the site of the 'Village' office block and of 1993s platforms Nos 18 and 19. New platform No 12 seems to be already in use for parcels traffic, although not open for passengers until August 1916. British Rail

22

Right:
Another view taken probably in May 1915 showing platforms Nos 17–21 in the 1885 Windsor line station realigned, reconstructed and equipped for electric traction. Platform No 16 is not quite ready and work is still in progress on extending the overall roof. The old alignment of the Windsor line platforms, seen in the foreground, would have obstructed the construction of the new arrival platforms Nos 12-15. Demolition of the 1860 roof over old platforms Nos 5-7 is in progress but the tracks are still in situ and the train of assorted vehicles in platform No 6 may indicate that parcels traffic was still being handled there.
Courtesy of the National Railway Museum

Below right:
The central cab roadway passed under the office block through this ornamental arch decorated with the LSWR crest in stained glass and stone panels listing the counties served by the company. The array of flags suggests that this picture was taken during the Victory celebrations in July 1919.
British Rail

Right:
Beyond the central archway construction work on the roof and office blocks had ceased soon after the outbreak of war. A wooden roof covers the concourse behind platforms Nos 12-21 and the refreshment room is also temporary pending the completion of the main buffet in the stone-faced section of the new buildings. British Rail.

Centre right:
Between platform No 15 and the wall of the Windsor line station the 'Village' block is under construction in 1919. This contained the stationmaster's office and various staff mess rooms and canteens. British Rail

Bottom right:
The stationmaster's office overlooked the escalators from the concourse to the Waterloo & City line installed in April 1919. These were of the original sideways-off type and were replaced by the straight comb design in 1935. The firmly closed shutters indicate that this was a Sunday when the 'Drain' did not operate.
Courtesy of the National Railway Museum.

Above:
The Royal limousine with
HM Queen Mary passes
through the gates of
Waterloo on 21 March
1922 after she had entered
through the Victory Arch
to open officially the rebuilt
station. In front of the arch
stands a guard of honour of
LSWR employees who had
distinguished themselves
while serving in the forces
during World War 1.
Courtesy of the National
Railway Museum

Right:
Seen on 13 July 1993, the
Victory Arch has been
cleaned and gilded. The
medallions above the
doorway bear the names of
the 1914-1918 theatres of
war, not the countries to be
served from the
International station whose
roof can be glimpsed
through the draught screen.
Brian Morrison

CHAPTER 2

The Southern Railway Era

'A' box still stood above the outer end of the platforms; it had been enlarged in 1910/11 and adapted to the new layout. The signals which formerly sprouted from the roof had been replaced by route indicators and most lines were now track circuited. The box's 16 signalmen worked 266 levers making 24,000 movements each day. The station approaches were controlled by the 100-lever 'B' box near the West Crossings and the 'C' cabin of 30 levers nearer Vauxhall. A disadvantage of the layout was the fact that up suburban trains had to cross the path of both up and down main line services outside Waterloo in order to reach their platforms Nos 1-4. This became a handicap to catering for the explosive growth in commuter traffic encouraged by electrification and the Southern Railway's publicity.

The solution was to transpose the tracks into Waterloo by means of a flyover at Durnsford Road near Wimbledon, which brought the two local lines together on the south side of the approach viaduct. This involved building a new platform at Vauxhall as well as a complete rearrangement of the layout leading to platforms Nos 1-6 at Waterloo. The track work at Waterloo was carried out within a single weekend. The flyover and the altered arrangement of tracks, together with colour light signalling from Vauxhall to New Malden came into use during a seven-hour stoppage on Sunday 17 May 1936. Temporary

A signalling plan shows the track rearrangement and the altered layout leading to platforms Nos 1-6 carried out in May 1936 but retaining temporary semaphore signals at Waterloo's three boxes.

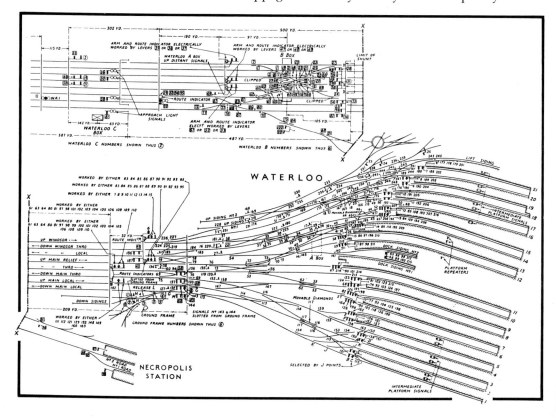

mechanical signalling remained in use at Waterloo during the summer of 1936.

The final stage of modernisation was the opening on 18 October 1936 of the new power box at Waterloo. Its three frames and 309 levers controlled all lines as far as Loco Junction at Nine Elms, replacing five mechanical boxes and completing the colour light signalling all the way from Waterloo to Hampton Court Junction. Some much needed additions could now be made to the electric suburban services.

Simultaneously the electrification was in progress of the main line to Portsmouth and the lines to Chertsey and Alton, with conversion taking place in stages during 1937. With the advent of main line electrification the remaining platforms at Waterloo (Nos 7-15) were equipped with the third-rail. Platforms Nos 7, 8 and 11 were lengthened and umbrella awnings erected beyond the overall roof at the end of platforms Nos 9-14. A new arrival indicator was installed in 1938; waiting travellers could pass the time in the News Cinema opened in August 1934 above the approach road near platform No 1 – this succumbed to the television age in 1970.

The small South side loco yard ceased to be used much after 1937 and its counterpart in the North sidings also became redundant after the Reading electrification of January 1939 banished regular steam passenger working from the Windsor side. Its turntable remained and was used for turning the 'Devon Belle' observation car during 1947-54.

World War 2 again brought heavy military traffic to Waterloo and this time enemy air raids caused much damage and disruption. Waterloo was fortunate in that its central structure did not suffer the destruction experienced by other SR termini. The worst effect was the loss of the old LSWR general offices, badly blasted in December 1940 and finally demolished in January 1941. The Southern's headquarters had been evacuated to Deepdene House, Dorking, at the outbreak of war. The site was cleared and eventually a typical 1960s office block was erected for the Department of Education. On the other side of the station the night of 16 April 1941 saw the destruction of the Necropolis station and the funeral train – a service never resumed. This site is now occupied by prefabricated buildings currently housing the driver training school for the former SR network. One of the longest closures of Waterloo followed the bombing of 10 May 1941 when thousands of gallons of precious bonded spirits blazed in the arches beneath the platforms.

Right:
W. H. Smith & Son published a series of picture postcards of the new station. This one shows suburban electric trains in platforms Nos 1-5. The hexagonal destination indicator above platform No 3 shows that the six-car electric is bound for Shepperton, but the presence of three three-car units in platform No 1 is surprising as normal formations were of three, six or eight cars.
Author's collection

Centre right:
A view from 'A' box taken about 1932 looking across the Windsor line station towards the South Bank. In platform No 13 a 'H15' 4-6-0 is waiting to run light to Nine Elms sheds, while a 'U1' 2-6-0 stands in platform No 14. A mixture of steam and electric stock is stabled in the North sidings.
Alan A. Jackson collection

Bottom right:
From the other side of 'A' box there was this view of Waterloo's approach tracks. At this date (1932) the lines into the main line platforms were not electrified. The 11 tracks cross Westminster Bridge Road on the skew, while beyond stand the buildings of Fields' soap and candle factory. Alan A. Jackson collection

Above:
The Southern Railway
proudly presented its new
express engine No 453
King Arthur *to its*
directors and the press at
Waterloo in February 1925.
Ian Allan Library

Right:
In September 1926 the new
4-6-0 No 850 Lord Nelson
leaves Waterloo on the
11.30am to Bournemouth
during running-in trials
from Eastleigh.
Ian Allan Library

Top left:
The scene in January 1935 overlooking the central roadway with its line of waiting taxis. A semi-fast train composed of ex LSWR lavatory stock stands at platform 10 shortly after arrival. A short boat train headed by a 'T9' waits to depart from platform No 8. The station's famous clock is an example of the SR's pioneer efforts to introduce the 24-hour system.
Southern Railway

Bottom left:
On a wet 30 March 1936 the elevated manual 'A' box and its semaphore signals had six and a half months of further use before being replaced by the power box nearing completion in the background.
Locomotive Publishing Co/IAL

Right:
During the installation in May 1936 of the new track layout outside platforms Nos 1-6, a 'Schools' 4-4-0 departs on the down through line with a Portsmouth train.
Courtesy of the National Railway Museum

Below right:
The 309 miniature levers in the new power box were arranged in three separate frames, one of which is seen here in February 1937. Magazine train describers on the shelf above communicated with the adjacent box at Nine Elms Loco Junction.
R. F. Roberts

32

Right:
The LSWR had installed mechanical departure indicators between platforms Nos 6 and 7 and on the Windsor side between Nos 18 and 19. During the ASLEF strike on 11 June 1955 the former could only offer three departures in the ensuing four hours. Denis Cullum

Below:
The Southern Railway installed a similar arrival indicator between platforms Nos 12 and 13 in 1938 which displays here the main line trains expected on 11 December 1964.
BR/C. J. Marsden
collection.

Right:
At the back of the main line booking office were the suburban ticket windows on the concourse, these were closed on 5 December 1970. Alan A. Jackson

Below:
The London Necropolis Co's station was situated in Westminster Bridge Road; from its courtyard mourners ascended to waiting rooms alongside the left hand platform. Coffins were loaded into the funeral vans at the right hand platform which were then attached by a 'M7' tank to the four ex-LSWR corridor coaches forming set No 99.   Lens of Sutton

Right:
The air raid of 5 January 1941 completed the destruction of the old LSWR general offices and also wrecked the passage linking the Windsor line concourse to the Bakerloo booking hall and lifts. Any damage to the Waterloo & City's Armstrong hoist behind would have been immaterial as the line was already at a standstill following the earlier bomb damage nearby.
British Rail

34

Right:
The contents of the bonded warehouses in the arches beneath Waterloo were set on fire during the heavy bombing of 10/11 May 1941. Two days later smoke is still rising through platforms Nos 12 and 13. The weakened arches had to be strengthened by steel girders before trains could use the station once more.
British Rail

Centre right:
A wartime scene recorded on 7 August 1942. No 865 Sir John Hawkins, *still in prewar malachite green livery, stands at the head of the second division of the 10.50am to the West of England while Drummond 'Paddlebox' 4-6-0 No 445 departs on the 10.54am semi-fast to Salisbury.*
Southern Railway.

Bottom right:
New 'Merchant Navy' Pacific No 21C8 has just been named Orient Line *by the chairman of the shipping company on 2 November 1942 and has coupled on to a West of England relief train. The stationmaster has donned his silk hat in honour of the occasion.*
Courtesy of the National Railway Museum

Right:
The return of peace found vast crowds trying to get away for summer holidays at a time when train services were still limited. On Saturdays the concourse and central roadway at Waterloo were packed solid with patient travellers hopefully standing in the correct queue for their destination, though the notice boards do not quote any departure times. Sometimes thousands more would be lined up in York Road just waiting to enter the station.
Courtesy of the National Railway Museum

Below right:
A quieter day for the terminus seen from the news cinema balcony just prior to nationalisation. A 1925 design 4-SUB unit is in platform No 4, BIL and HAL two-car units form a Portsmouth/Alton electric in platform No 6, with a 4-COR unit behind on a Portsmouth fast train. A 'Lord Nelson' has arrived with what appears to be a boat train. Glass has been restored to most of the overall roof, but passengers are reminded that cheap day return tickets are not available from Waterloo between 4.30 and 6.30pm.
Courtesy of the National Railway Museum.

36

Right:
On 24 October 1946 Urie 'King Arthur' No 742 Camelot, *newly restored to the malachite green livery, awaits the loading of large quantities of mail into the 10.54am semi-fast to Salisbury. Wartime blackout material still covers the station roof and all the glass has been removed from the vertical screen, which seems to have lost some of its structure.*
G. J. Jefferson

Centre right:
The ruins of the LSWR general offices have been cleared away and the site roughly tidied up when seen in 1948. The canopy over the cab road to the left of the Victory Arch was extended at this time, ostensibly for the benefit of boat train travellers.
Courtesy of the National Railway Museum

Bottom right:
The centenary of Waterloo station was celebrated on 11 July 1948 by the restoration of Adams 'T3' 4-4-0 563 and a tri-composite coach to LSWR livery for a brief ceremony and exhibition at platform No 15. Fittingly, the 80-year old Sir Herbert Walker was present. Both engine and carriage can now be seen together in the National Railway Museum.
Ian Allan Library.

CHAPTER 3

The Postwar Years

hen Waterloo station modestly celebrated its centenary
on 11 July 1948 it still bore the scars of war, but in 1951 the South
Bank became the site of the Festival of Britain exhibition and
Waterloo received some much needed renovation. The
development of the South Bank's cultural complex led to the
erection of a high level walkway from the Windsor line
concourse in October 1965. Following the end of steam traction
at Waterloo on 9 July 1967, train crew accommodation at Nine
Elms was transferred to a raft built above the buffer stops of
platforms Nos 1-6.

The modernisation of Waterloo's passenger facilities began on
6 December 1970 when a new 16 window ticket office was
opened opposite platforms Nos 13-15 on the site of the former
'Long Bar' refreshment room. This replaced the main line
booking hall and the two suburban offices on the concourse. The
site of the old booking hall could then become in May 1973 a
new restaurant, the 'Great Express', later to become the
'Trafalgar Buffet' and 'Trips' coffee house as it progressed down
the path to self-service. This replaced the first floor Surrey Room
restaurant, which became a staff canteen, and the Windsor tea
room. Already, in 1972 the circular buffet opposite platform No
11, (latterly the 'Horseshoe Bar') had become the 'Drum' and in
1980 it joined the fast-food market as a 'Casey Jones'.

In January 1977 the disused Windsor tea room was converted
into a large travel centre, but happily the decorative cashiers
kiosks were retained to display publicity material. To conclude
the tale of Waterloo's catering facilities; the Windsor line buffet
has been transformed into 'Bonaparte', a privately-operated up-
market coffee house. At the other end of the station the former
gentlemen's lavatory opposite platform 2 (described by the
Railway Magazine as 'the finest in England' when it opened in
1910) was converted in 1987 into a French bistro, which closed in
1993 before it could welcome through travellers from Paris.
Refurbishment of the remaining toilets in 1986 involved a
tenfold increase in the price of 'spending a penny'.

Outside on the concourse other changes were taking place.
During 1977 the Bostick gates were removed from the platform
entrances and replaced by a new barrier line incorporating
various shops and kiosks which hide the trains from view.
Above were installed three Solari departure indicators (the
Windsor line one has since disappeared) with linked destination
signs in the subway and at platform gates. More recently, dot
matrix displays have been added to inform the public of special
messages and train alterations. These can also substitute for the
Solari equipment, which has never been as reliable as the two
mechanical departure indicators installed by the LSWR.
Waterloo was a pioneer in the use of loud speakers for train
announcements as far back as 1932 and the grey years of the war
were enlivened by broadcasting cheerful music to the concourse.

The station announcer was situated in a glass eyrie on the roof of the stationmaster's office.

The 1980s saw the cleaning of the brickwork and stone facings of the office buildings and slowly the concourse flooring was replaced by terrazzo paving, giving the terminus a bright and fresh appearance. The Victory arch was provided with glazed screens, so removing 'pneumonia corner' from the Windsor line concourse. One matter for regret; to discourage vagrants sleeping overnight, the benches on the concourse have been replaced by concrete blocks to which tilting plastic misericordes are attached. The gloomy passage and stairs leading to the Colonnade bus stops in Waterloo Road was also refurbished with Lambeth Council financial help. Retail facilities have been transformed with bright boutiques and a walk-around W. H. Smith shop (one of the old bookstalls is preserved on the North Norfolk Railway), but the post office has gone.

Operating facilities also changed during the 1980s; platforms Nos 1-4 were shortened to allow simpler trackwork to be installed and there was a realignment of track into platforms Nos 9-14 to give improved clearances and to remove redundant pointwork. A new double crossover at Vauxhall between Fast

The cover of a publicity leaflet issued by the Southern Region in the late-1950s carried this aerial view of the station. The difference in the pattern of roofing is noticeable between the concourse, the main line platforms and the Windsor line station. Even the canopy over the cab road shows the variation of the 1948 extension near the Victory arch. The ruins of the LSWR general offices have been cleared away and the road pattern altered for the 1951 Festival of Britain, but no office development has yet taken place along York Road. The turntable in the North sidings remains and there seem to be two tank wagons in the nearby sidings, perhaps dating this picture to the 1951-54 period of main line diesel operation. At the left of the picture a steam loco makes its way from Ewer Street depot towards Charing Cross.

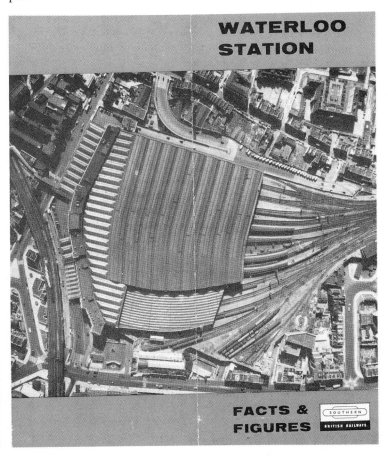

WATERLOO STATION

FACTS & FIGURES

SOUTHERN BRITISH RAILWAYS

Right:
For the 1951 Festival of Britain the general office bomb site was beautified and a screen carrying the first BR crest concealed the blank wall at the side of the Victory Arch. Seen here on 18 June 1953 the entrance to the station has been decorated for the Coronation of HM the Queen. Denis Cullum.

Below:
The other major casualty at Waterloo from enemy bombing was the Necropolis station. After clearance of the ruins, the site was occupied by these prefabricated offices used for staff planning the Kentish electrification schemes. 'West Country' Pacific No 34007 Wadebridge is seen passing with the 14.54 to Salisbury on 4 June 1965. P. H. Groom

and Slow lines replaced part of the West crossings. All this arose from the urgent need to replace the life-expired frames and wiring in the 1936 box with a temporary operating panel linked to a local relay room on the site of the former North turntable. This was done during the weekend of 5 February 1984. Meanwhile Department of Transport approval was awaited for a complete resignalling of the lines out of Waterloo. When authorised in 1986 this was intended as an inexpensive replacement of old equipment on a 'like for like' basis, but the designation of Waterloo as the terminal for Channel Tunnel services soon brought major changes to the plans.

Right:
During the mid-1950s Urie 'H16' 4-6-2T leaves platform No 13 with empty stock for Clapham Yard, while trains of EPB stock arrive off the up through line and depart from the Windsor side for that destination. The Festival of Britain exhibition buildings on the South Bank have disappeared except for the entrance hall then being used as British European Airways town terminal. The later Windsor line loco yard and turntable can be seen to the left of No 30520's steam.
Ian Allan Library

Centre right:
A block of flats on the site of the old Fields' factory provides a superb vantage point for photographers. Even the bomb-damaged building in the foreground was to disappear in later years. The power box is on the left with the Westminster Bridge Road cab entrance below. On 5 September 1966 BR Standard Class 4 4-6-0 No 75069 leaves with the 17.09 to Basingstoke. J. Scrace

Bottom right:
The different forms of traction to be seen at Waterloo during the 1960s are shown here on 11 December 1965 with No 34098 Templecombe on an up Bournemouth express in platform No 13, 'Warship' diesel No D820 Grenville on an Exeter train in platform No 14 and 4-SUB unit No 4123 in No 15. R. E. Ruffell

Above:
As No 35023 enters Waterloo on 8 July 1967 with the last steam-hauled Channel Islands boat train, No 41319 and a 'Warship' diesel occupy the dock roads, while a push-pull fitted 'Crompton' (probably No D6529) heads a van train in platform No 12. A few spotters record their last steam sightings at Waterloo.
J. H. Cooper-Smith

Right:
For a few years after its completion the viewing gallery at the top of the Shell building provided photographers with a birds-eye view of Waterloo. On 7 September 1971 a 12 car REP/TC formation from Bournemouth is entering platform No 11, while a 'Warship' is waiting to depart in platform No 10 for Exeter and a 4-CIG on a Portsmouth train is in No 8. The Windsor line turntable has been removed, but the North loco sidings remain and appear to contain a Class 74 electro-diesel.
J. H. Cooper-Smith

Right:
Following the end of steam traction, train crew mess rooms and offices were transferred to a raft above platforms Nos 1-6, from which staff could observe activity on the platforms. On 28 February 1977 this provided a view of a variety of VEP, CIG, REP, EPB and 4-SUB units.
R. E. Ruffell

Centre right:
The 14 (originally 16) windows of the new ticket office installed on the concourse in December 1970 have not brought an end to queues.
Stephen C. Morris

Bottom right:
Three Solari departure indicators were installed above the new barrier line in 1977 — over the Suburban and Windsor line platforms and this main display over platforms No 12-15, which also incorporates estimated main line arrival times. The hexagonal kiosk dispenses tourist rather than train information.
Brian Morrison

44

Right:
*Seen on 4 November 1977
is the control panel for the
new Solari indicators and
the closed circuit television
screens monitoring the
platforms.* R. E. Ruffell

Below:
*A close-up of activity on the
evening of 13 May 1980. A
TC/REP formation is
entering platform No 12 via
the up main relief line,
while two VEP units come
off the up through.
Simultaneously two Class
508 units are arriving on
the up local line.*
J. G. Glover

Above:
The approaches to Waterloo are seen from an incoming suburban train on 16 April 1977. An Exeter departure hauled by a Class 33 diesel has reached the start of the West crossings, protected by the signal gantry above.
Alan A. Jackson

Right:
During the 1980s the concourse buildings and flooring were cleaned and refurbished giving the station this light and attractive appearance seen on 24 July 1985.
Alan A. Jackson

46

Right:
On the site of the demolished LSWR offices and along the York Road frontage, the 1960s saw the construction of these office blocks for the Department of Education. The Windsor line platforms and the North sidings are also seen in this view from the power box on 25 February 1977. R. E. Ruffell

Centre right:
The pre-fab buildings on the site of the Necropolis station have been refurbished since the earlier picture was taken in 1965 and now house the Driving Training School, with unit No 465203 on hand to provide practice on 'Networker' stock. When seen on 14 November 1992, No 73006 was arriving with the stock of the 09.30 'Mule & Otter Axeman' rail tour. Brian Morrison

Bottom right:
Looking in the other direction from the Canterbury House flats on 14 November 1992, Class 33/2 No 33202 departs from Waterloo International station with a ballast train and joins the NSE lines at International Junction. Above the train can be seen the West crossings linking the approach lines outside the terminus. Brian Morrison

CHAPTER 4

The Coming of the International Station

T he 1936 signal-box itself was an obstacle to the construction of the new International station and on 30 September 1990 its panel was transferred to a small temporary building near the relay room. This in turn was demolished after control of the Waterloo area was taken over by the Wimbledon signalling centre on 2 April 1991. In contrast to 1936, these changes involved a full weekend's blockade, with the only traffic in and out of Waterloo being two electric trains shuttling to and from Clapham Junction on one pair of tracks under pilotman working. Unlike other ex-SR termini there is no alternative to Waterloo and it must stay open if at all possible.

Since 1909 the eight tracks between Vauxhall and Waterloo had been divided into three Windsor and five Main. In the absence of any widening of the viaduct through Vauxhall, the up Windsor line had to be converted to bi-directional use for Channel Tunnel traffic. Between Vauxhall and Waterloo up Windsor line trains now take the former down Windsor through line and the present two down Windsor lines occupy the original down Windsor local and up Main relief lines. Beyond a series of parallel crossovers near the West crossings, known as Carlisle Lane Junction, the up Main relief resumes as a short reversible line serving platforms Nos 8-17. The tracks into the International station diverge from the Windsor lines at International Junction, slightly nearer Waterloo. The new crossovers at Waterloo, Vauxhall and Nine Elms were laid in during the winter of 1990/91 and came into use for NSE traffic with the new signalling.

The International station was planned to occupy the site of the 1885 Windsor line platforms. Before these could be demolished, alternative accommodation had to be found for NSE services. The first stage was to build two long platforms on the site of the dock sidings and the roadway between platforms Nos 11 and 12. These came into use on 2 July 1990 and were numbered 12 and 13; existing platforms Nos 12-15 then became Nos 14-17. Already demolition was in progress on the Windsor station and when two short platforms, Nos 18 and 19 at the outer end of the 'Village' block were ready on 3 December 1990, the remaining platforms in the old station (Nos 19-21) could be handed over to the contractors. When construction work was completed, platforms Nos 18 and 19 were extended towards the concourse to their full length.

Waterloo has thus suffered the loss of two platforms and one of its approach tracks, but the virtual ending of parcels, newspaper and mail traffic in 1988 and the elimination of loco haulage in 1993, coupled with the effect of the recession on NSE traffic, has avoided any congestion.

One of the first effects of the International station work was the closure of the subway linking the main line platforms to the York Road entrance. Part of the Windsor line concourse

Far right:
A signalling and track diagram shows the present layout of the NSE station following the platform changes in 1990 and the transfer of control to the Wimbledon signalling centre in April 1991. Access from the Up Main Slow is to platforms Nos 1-7, from the Up Fast to Nos 5-15, from the reversible Up Main Relief to Nos 8-17 and from the Up Windsor and Windsor Reversible lines to Nos 14-19. Departure to the Down Main Slow is from platforms Nos 1-7, to the Down Fast from Nos 5-15, to the Down Windsor lines from Nos 8-19 and to the Windsor Reversible from Nos 14-19.

The 1885 Windsor line station was to be the site of the new International terminal, entailing the demolition of the century-old building and the attractive ironwork of its roof. A mixture of VEP and Class 455 stock is in the platforms on 24 March 1988. Brian Morrison

cleared late in 1990 and the rest raised on to a raft for a year while offices for the International station were built underneath. Before the 'Village' block could be demolished, its inhabitants, including the Station Manager, had to be housed with other staff on a large new raft spanning platforms Nos 1-10. The International station is expected to attract considerable road traffic and to avoid interrupting the flow of vehicles, the pedestrian crossing linking the South Western terminus with the footbridge to the South Eastern station was replaced in January 1993 by a high level walkway which emerges above the main concourse through the site of the Surrey Room restaurant, with a lift, escalators and stairs to concourse level. The NSE headquarters staff who had used the Surrey Room as a canteen have been transferred to a modern office block in Blackfriars Road. Meanwhile the old LSWR office accommodation at Waterloo has been extensively refurbished.

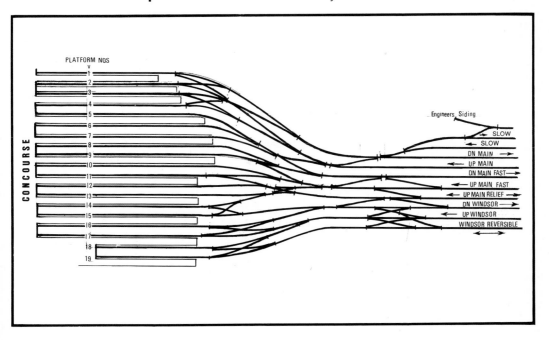

Waterloo station 1922-1993

	1922 Main line station			1993 NSE station	
Span	Platform	Length(ft)	Out of use	Into use	Length(ft)
1	1	696			571
	2	695			572
	3	683			580
2	4	685			580
	5	720			702
	6	723			723
	7	728			798
3	8	735			805
	9	756			827
	10	765			837
	11	860			817
4 Dock	1	160	1/89		
Cab roadway			(new) 12	2/7/90	825
			(new) 13	2/7/90	830
Dock	2	175	2/90		
5	12	843	renumbered 14	2/7/90	843
	13	857	renumbered 15	2/7/90	857
	14	860	renumbered 16	2/7/90	860
	15	635	renumbered 17	2/7/90	869

6 The 'Village' office block – demolished 3/91 onwards

				Into use	Length(ft)
			(new) 18	} 3/12/90 outer part	804
			(new) 19	} 4/10/93 remainder	804

Windsor line (North) station

	Platform	Length(ft)	Out of use
	16	570	2/3/90
	17	600	30/6/90
	18	612	30/6/90
	19	605	30/11/90
	20	625	30/11/90
	21	551	30/11/90 (already disused)

Note:
Platform 11 was 946ft long between 1937 and 1984.

Right:
A feature of the Windsor Line station was the turret above platform No 21 which marked the original end of the overall roof before this was extended in 1915. On 29 June 1973 4-SUB units are stabled in the north sidings. R. E. Ruffell

Below:
The 1936 power box was built above the arches leading from Westminster Bridge Road to the cab roadway which emerged on the south side of the station. Cleaning of the stonework had revealed in February 1988 the original LSWR inscription over the entrance. The local authority had recently sponsored this example of popular art to cover the blank wall below the signalbox. Author

Right:
The dock roads between platforms Nos 11 and 12, seen here on 7 October 1974, had ceased to be required for parcel traffic or for a Class 09 station pilot. They could therefore, form the basis for the other two extra platforms needed to replace the Windsor line station. Brian Morrison

Facing page, top:
The 1936 signal box was demolished in October 1990 after the operating panel had been transferred to a temporary building near the 1984 relay room. In this picture taken on 7 December 1990 the temporary building is the small lit structure behind the wooden stockade. Within the contractors' area work is starting on the removal of the last of the Windsor line platforms, which have just been replaced by the new platforms Nos 18 and 19. A Class 455 unit is leaving from one of the platforms in the main station now being used for Windsor line traffic. C. J. Marsden

Facing page, bottom:
Behind the dock roads was the central cab roadway with its slope from Griffin Street. The taxi rank was now located in front of the station, mail and parcel traffic was minimal after 1988, so that this roadway was excavated to form the base for the new platforms; the work is seen here on 18 February 1989.
Alan A. Jackson

54

Right:
The two new platforms came into use on 2 July 1990 and are seen here two days later with some very temporary labelling. All the platforms beyond had consequently to have their numbers increased by two. Alan A. Jackson

Centre right:
The other two new platforms were Nos 18 and 19, whose outer portions were brought into use on 3 December 1990. Due to the building works still taking place in the area of the former 'Village' block, these platforms were mainly used during the rush hours. On 6 July 1993 Class 455/7 unit No 5723 on the 10.43 service to Windsor & Eton Riverside stands in platform No 17 (the former No 15), while units Nos 5734 and 5852 form the 10.46 to Weybridge via Hounslow in platform No 15 (once main line arrival platform No 13). Brian Morrison

Bottom right:
The first train to enter Waterloo International was an engineer's rake of ZGV 'Seacows' with Class 33/2 No 33202 The Burma Star on 14 November 1992. Class 455/7 unit No 5732 leaves with the 09.32 Kingston Roundabout service, while a Class 442 'Wessex' unit departs simultaneously for Weymouth. Unusually, a Class 60 can be seen in Waterloo at the head of a rail tour special. The view from Canterbury House has changed much since steam enthusiasts found their way to its balconies in the 1960s. Brian Morrison

CHAPTER 5

Waterloo (East)

This station was opened by the SER on 1 January 1869 as Waterloo Junction, in succession to its shortlived Blackfriars station near Blackfriars Road. It was not a junction used by regular passenger traffic and ceased to be a junction at all in 1911, but the Junction title lingered until 7 July 1935. The station then became just 'Waterloo' but could be distinguished from the main terminal by the designation of its four platforms as A to D. Eventually on 8 May 1978 it became known officially as Waterloo (East). Originally intended for the exchange of commuter traffic with the LSWR, Waterloo Junction was only gradually served by main line trains, a process completed in July 1933 when the SR introduced stops there by the 80min Folkestone expresses.

When opened the station had three platforms, but a fourth was added to the south side on 2 June 1901. At this period the four platforms were arranged – up, down, down, up; the northern pair being for trains running via Cannon Street and the southern for those routed direct to London Bridge. This arrangement had the advantage that all down trains used the central island platform. The practice of running in and out of Cannon Street ceased during World War 1, so in 1925 the four tracks were rearranged into local and through line pairs. Platforms A and B to the north served the local lines, C and D on the south side the through lines. This was a preliminary to electrification which took place in stages commencing on 28 February 1926.

The congested tracks between London Bridge and Charing Cross were often affected by fog; these conditions caused the worst accident to take place in the Waterloo area, when three passengers lost their lives in a rear-end collision between Blackheath and Mid-Kent trains near Waterloo Junction on 25 October 1913. Colour light signalling replaced Sykes 'Lock & Block' mechanical working at the time of electrification in 1926.

This pioneer installation was replaced in 1976 as part of the London Bridge resignalling scheme. At Waterloo Solari indicators on the footbridge and platforms were intended to inform passengers of impending departures, but never quite managed to provide an answer to the question 'does the next train to Charing Cross leave from platform B or platform D?' The footbridge, damaged by fire in 1965, was refurbished and the ticket office modernised. In 1984 the Greater London Council partially financed further improvements on the platforms (where part of the awnings were removed) and on the footbridge, where several shops were added to serve the commuters hurrying between South Western and South Eastern sections. All this was, however, in vain, as the construction of the high level walkway has swept away the shops, closed the ticket office and removed the remaining traces of the junction line.

Facing page, top:
The top floor of the offices above the main terminus provided a birds-eye view of the erstwhile Waterloo Junction station, seen here on 14 June 1962. The former connection to the LSWR followed the awning in the right hand corner.
J. Scrace

Facing page, bottom:
A fire on the Eastern footbridge in 1965 opened up a closer view (taken on 24 April) of the facade of the main line terminus. The footbridge linking the two stations is on the left with a surviving fragment of the the New Waterloo platform marking the course of the connecting line. Author

58

Right:
'West Country' No 34020
Seaton *approaches*
Waterloo East *with the*
Saturday 10.52am Charing
Cross-Deal on 6 August
1960. Beyond the York
Road roundabout the
downstream Shell building
is nearly complete. On the
up side of the viaduct is the
site of the Belvedere Road
turntable, where some of
the railway exhibits were
displayed during the
Festival of Britain.
J. C. Beckett

Below:
Steam traction could still be
seen at Waterloo East
during 1960; here 'Schools'
No 30924 Haileybury is
seen on 4 May with the
11.46am passenger and
parcels train from Charing
Cross to Ashford. J. Scrace

Right:
During the interim stage between steam and full electric traction, many Charing Cross services were diesel hauled; on 1 April 1961 during the heating season, Derby/Sulzer Bo-Bo No D5013 provides both haulage and warmth for the 4.10pm Charing Cross-Ramsgate. Progress on the Shell tower in the background can be compared with the previous picture. Author.

Centre right:
At a time when the EPB stock is about to disappear from the South Eastern lines, here is a glimpse of the pre-EPB era at Waterloo East on 16 July 1955. A 4-SUB unit heads the Dartford Loop train at platform A, the HAL two-car unit in platform C is bound for Gillingham, while a four-car unit of LSWR origin at platform D may have arrived from Caterham or Tattenham Corner. Alan A. Jackson

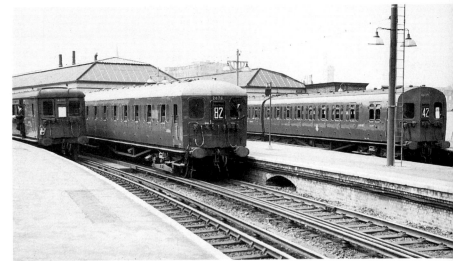

Bottom right:
Looking from the footbridge, the line towards Charing Cross passes through a canyon between the two Shell buildings. The down train approaching platform A on 24 April 1965 is bound for Bromley North, a destination no longer served by through trains from Waterloo. Author

60

Above:
Until the advent of the 'Networker' stock the only sliding door units seen at Waterloo East were the Class 455s on the off-peak Charing Cross-Caterham service. Unit No 5804 is leaving platform C (the normal one for this route) on 17 September 1987. Platform awnings have been cut back as part of the refurbishment of the station. Author

Right:
Waterloo East station seen from the section of the footbridge which has not been modernised. Class 465/0 'Networker' units Nos 465002/012 provide modern traction for the 15.52 Sevenoaks-Charing Cross on 28 May 1993. Brian Morrison

Above:
The new high level
footbridge linking the East
station to the main line
terminus across Waterloo
Road gives the impression
of an aircraft fuselage.
Below it remains the
structure of the old bridge,
now stripped of its roof,
while in the background the
skew girder bridge carries
the lines to Charing Cross.
Brian Morrison

Right:
The link from the East
station descends by stairs
and escalators to the main
line concourse through the
site of the Surrey Room
restaurant. Its successor,
the 'Casey Jones' burger bar
can be seen on the left.
Brian Morrison

CHAPTER 6

The Underworld

Since Waterloo station was built on a viaduct, the space beneath its platforms was soon occupied by a network of arches and tunnels, many dark and evil-smelling from the passage of horse-drawn cabs and carts. Under platform No 10 in the North station was the milk arch, scarcely any more inviting, where churns arriving from the West Country were dispatched to London's dairies.

The advent of the underground railway brought deeper excavations beneath the terminus. The Waterloo & City Railway had its separate arrival and departure platforms at right angles to the main line tracks within four of the supporting arches. Slopes and stairs linked the W&C to the South station concourse, to platforms Nos 3 and 4 in the Central station and to the north end of the Windsor line station. The W&C sidings, depot and power house were originally in the open between the old South station and Lower Marsh, but came to be almost entirely buried after the construction of the new South extension and its approach roads. The Waterloo & City was formally opened by HRH the Duke of Cambridge on 11 July 1898 (the 50th anniversary of the main line terminus) and public services started on 8 August 1898.

The W&C power station provided lighting supply to the main line station during the early stages of rebuilding, but following LSWR suburban electrification, the W&C supply was taken from the LSWR large generating station at Durnsford Road, Wimbledon. Originally fed by a central conductor rail at 500V, the W&C was converted to the SR's standard 600V outside third-rail supply in October 1940. New trains and automatic colour-light signalling were other features of this modernisation. The

Finishing touches are being made to the Waterloo & City Railway platforms in 1898. The constraint of building within the existing arches supporting the main line terminus made it neccesary to have separate arrival and departure platforms, though a combined arch spanned the connections to the reversing siding and the depot roads. Courtesy of the National Railway Museum

gloomy platforms and bare brickwork gradually gave way to
brighter surroundings during the postwar years. In 1986 terazzo
paving installed on the platforms incorporated the NSE stripes
to guide the well-drilled commuting crowds to wait where the
car doors would open.

In 1985/86 the W&C depot was remodelled to undertake all
routine overhauls of the line's stock. Hitherto, cars had been
maintained at either Eastleigh works or Selhurst depot and were
lifted in and out of the tube by the Armstong hoist situated in
the north sidings beyond the Windsor line station. On 13 April
1948 Drummond 'M7' tank No 672 fell into the pit of this hoist
and had to be cut up on the spot. The hoist was demolished in
October 1990 to make way for the International station and the
W&C had to make the most of its surviving 50-year old stock
until further modernisation could take place. In July 1993 new
trains of LUL Central Line design were introduced, working off
the standard Underground four-rail system and with the benefit
of the latest signalling equipment. The changeover of stock was
effected via a hole above the depot near Lower Marsh, but
normally the new trains will remain underground for the whole
of their working life.

As the new station was completed from 1909 onwards its
platforms were linked by stairs to a long passage which
connected with the W&C platforms and the Bakerloo booking
hall and eventually to York Road. Part of this subway was used
as a free buffet for servicemen between December 1915 and April
1920. Other passages linked the W&C to Waterloo Road and the
concourse, their walls broken by little doorways leading to lost
property stores, staff clubs and canteens, a rifle range and the
police office – somewhere down here was the accommodation
provided for emigrants when the LSWR decided in 1913 that it
did not want them in the waiting rooms of its new station.

Having emerged from prolonged financial troubles, the Baker
Street & Waterloo Railway (the Bakerloo tube) was opened to
Waterloo on 10 March 1906. After several changes of plan, its
station was below the northern edge of the LSWR terminus on a
sharp curve as the line swung round from beneath the river to
continue towards Lambeth North. Lifts linked the platforms
with a booking hall at street level, from which a slope led to the
Windsor line concourse and a passage to York Road.

As part of the modernisation and expansion of the Hampstead
and City & South London tubes to create today's Northern Line,
the Underground Group extended the Hampstead tube from
Charing Cross to Kennington via Waterloo on 13 September
1926. The two new platforms and the Bakerloo ones were
connected to a new sub-surface booking hall by a bank of three
escalators. From there tube passengers could reach the SR
concourse via the existing 1919 escalators, or the main line
platforms through the long subway. To cater for the extra traffic

generated by the Festival of Britain in 1951, the passages between the Northern and Bakerloo lines were enlarged to form a low-level circulating area, while new escalators and stairs were built to a separate station entrance on the South Bank side of York Road.

In September 1970 two more escalators to the main line terminus were added in a separate shaft and when an enlarged ticket hall was completed in March 1973, the original Bakerloo lifts and booking office were taken out of service. The 1980s saw considerable refurbishment of the station and alterations to the ticket hall as part of the automatic fare collection project. Most of these changes at sub-surface level were shortlived as the whole area has been reconstructed to form the spacious new booking hall needed to cater for traffic from the International station. Part of this new booking hall came into use in July 1993.

Below right:
A view in the opposite direction taken on 7 March 1953 shows the berthing and depot roads enlarged in the early 1900s when most of the yard was covered by the girders supporting the new South station.
Alan A. Jackson

Below:
The Armstrong hoist in the North sidings behind platform No 21 was the means of transferring rolling stock to and from the Waterloo & City and also for lowering coal wagons to supply its generating plant, until this was superseded by the Durnsford Road station.
Author

Right:
W&C motor coach No 56 waits to be shunted on to the Armstrong hoist on 20 August 1981, having arrived from overhaul at Selhurst behind electro-diesel loco No 73003 with two SR bogie brake vans and a pair of match trucks.
C. J. Marsden

Right:
A train of the 1940 stock stands in the arrival platform at Waterloo in February 1986, prior to the NSE-image refurbishment soon to be carried out to trains and stations.
Colin Boocock

Below:
A view inside the re-equipped depot with some of the refurbished cars on 6 September 1992.
C. J. Marsden

68

Right:
Briefly during the changeover in May 1993, both 1940 and 1993 (Class 482) stock could be seen together in the depot sidings. C. J. Marsden

Centre right:
New Class 482 unit No 482509 stands in the arrival platform at Waterloo with a train from the Bank on 23 July 1993. Note that the NSE stripes on the platform do not match the door openings on this stock. Brian Morrison

Bottom right:
The London Underground ticket hall and concourse have been enlarged to cope with the expected traffic from the International station. More escalators are under construction from the concourse to the Northern Line and the anticipated advent of the Jubilee Line has been allowed for by a blank space in the direction signs. This view taken on 23 July 1993 shows how one of the LSWR arches below the Windsor line station has been opened up and its brickwork repointed to provide additional access from the ticket office to the escalators. Brian Morrison

CHAPTER 7

Trains and Traffic

A t 4.30am on 11 July 1848 the engine *Hornet* brought the Southampton mail train into the new Waterloo Bridge terminus. Maybe *Hornet* did not enter the station, as the practice in the early days at Waterloo was for the incoming train to stop at the ticket platform beyond Westminster Bridge Road. A rope was attached to the front coupling, the engine started off, the rope was released and while the loco entered a siding the carriages rolled into the platform. Such casual methods and the hand operation of points were adequate for the 70 trains which arrived and departed daily in 1848.

By 1867, with three times as much traffic, trains were being hauled all the way into the station under the protection of fixed signals. In 1869 the halt outside the terminus to collect tickets was replaced by the examination of incoming trains at Vauxhall, where a large staff of ticket collectors was employed in order to check a crowded train within the two minutes allowed. The old Waterloo was open to all comers and was the haunt of idlers and petty criminals. Gradually, the introduction of corridor stock and progress in the completion of the new platforms at Waterloo equipped with ticket barriers finally ended examination at Vauxhall by 1916.

Jerome K. Jerome's *Three Men in a Boat* found Waterloo a scene of chaotic activity – 'We got to Waterloo at eleven and asked where the eleven-five started from. Of course nobody knew; nobody at Waterloo ever does know where a train is going to start from, or where a train when it does start is going to, or anything about it.' Not surprisingly, the public got lost at Waterloo – the three separate stations, the South Western's practice of numbering platforms rather than faces and the absence of numbers for the two platforms in the South station. During the rush hour a main line express leaving from platforms Nos 1 or 2 might be preceded by a local to Kingston or Chertsey.

Class T9 No 307 leaving Waterloo with a special train, probably for the 1902 Coronation Naval Review at Spithead. Between the South sidings and the train is the down local road added in 1900.
Courtesy of the National Railway Museum

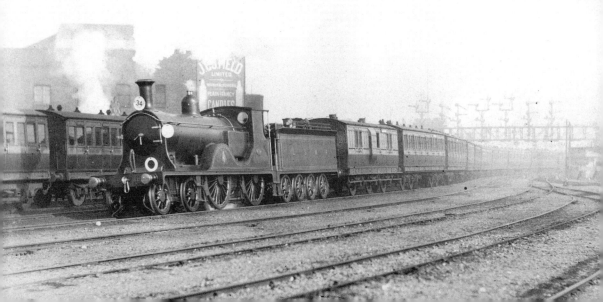

With only limited sidings at Waterloo, the terminus was dependent on a flow of empty stock to and from Clapham Junction or Wimbledon. When the additional lines were provided in 1891, the new up through was reserved for empty trains which waited outside the terminus until a platform was available. Although the through service to the SER had ceased in 1868, the LNWR ran services from Willesden to Waterloo between July 1875 and December 1892. The connecting line remained in use for special traffic and Queen Victoria passed over it on 22 March 1900 *en route* from Windsor to Woolwich to review troops leaving for the Boer War. A well-known popular print claims to depict the departure of troops for Southampton from platform No 1. In fact the despatch of the Brigade of Guards from Waterloo in October 1899 was accompanied by such unruly patriotic enthusiasm that later contingents left from the seclusion of Nine Elms.

The LSWR was always termed the 'military line' and the summer manoeuvres of the Volunteer or Territorial forces saw numerous troop trains leaving Waterloo. The Spithead naval reviews which marked the Coronation celebrations of 1902 and 1911 found the South Western's resources fully stretched to convey the assembled dignitaries to their ships in the allotted time. All the specials in 1911 were able to depart from the newly-completed South station. These were the years when major race meetings would require the LSWR to convey as many as 14,000 spectators, while Gold Cup day at Ascot would see 40 special trains from Waterloo.

For much of the duration of World War 1, Waterloo had to operate under the handicap of a mixture of old and new platforms. On Sunday evenings as many as 20 special trains would take the troops back to camp after weekend leave in the Metropolis. During the latter part of the war the Southampton-Havre route was the only Cross-Channel service available for civilian travellers and extra offices had to be provided at Waterloo to deal with bookings. Many servicemen on leave from France or other theatres of war reached Waterloo from Southampton and LSWR clerks manned kiosks to change grubby foreign money into Treasury notes.

During the war the inner suburban services were electrified on Sir Herbert Walker's principle of frequent trains at regular intervals. The outer suburban steam-worked services had to conform to the same pattern and in the postwar reorganisation of the main line timetable standard departure times to Portsmouth, Bournemouth and the West of England were fixed. Platforms in the rebuilt station could thus be allocated to departures for specific routes; main line arrivals were mostly handled at platforms Nos 13 and 14, whence the empty stock could easily leave for Clapham Yard via the down Windsor local line. July 1925 saw the electrification of the New Guildford and

The American Line was the first major Transatlantic service to adopt Southampton as its UK terminal and in 1893 the LSWR provided the 'Eagle' lavatory stock for its boat specials. One of these trains is seen here in platform No 1 at Waterloo close to its departure time of 8.30am.
Courtesy of the National Railway Museum

Leatherhead lines, so that steam traction was banished from platforms Nos 1-5 during the daytime. The line to Windsor was converted in 1930, leaving the Reading services as the only steam trains using the North station.

Long distance services were being improved and accelerated with the introduction of the powerful 'King Arthur' and 'Lord Nelson' 4-6-0s. On 19 July 1926 the principal 11.00am service to the West of England was named the 'Atlantic Coast Express' and in 1929 the restoration of two-hour trains to Bournemouth was marked by the introduction of the 'Bournemouth Limited', followed in 1931 by the all-Pullman 'Bournemouth Belle'.

Equally prestigious were the Ocean Liner Expresses to and from Southampton Docks, which included Pullman cars in their formation from 1931 onwards. During the 1950s the most important trains, those conveying the first class and Pullman travellers, acquired such names as 'Cunarder', 'Statesman' or 'Springbok'. Platform No 11 was normally left free for boat trains; nearest to the buffers would be two large vans, from which arriving passengers' baggage was unloaded into an alphabetically labelled compound between the train and the central taxi roadway. The British Transport award-winning film *Terminus* made in 1960 shows the famous and the fashionable leaving Waterloo by boat train. It also features the less glamorous departure from platform 11 of a party of convicts bound for Dartmoor prison in the front coach of the 9.00am to Plymouth, a once regular working.

The interwar years saw a growth in holiday traffic concentrated on the Saturdays around the August Bank Holiday period. Offices still worked on Saturday mornings then, so Waterloo had to cope simultaneously with commuters as well as holidaymakers. Empty trains formed of older stock kept in suburban sidings stood on the up relief line waiting to enter the terminus. To save line occupation between Waterloo and Loco Junction, light engines to and from Nine Elms coupled together in convoys. Sometimes it was easier to send them to the depot via Clapham Junction and the low level lines at Nine Elms to avoid crossing the main lines outside Waterloo.

The key to such movements was the West crossings, a series of double slip connections, formerly controlled by the old 'B' box, which enabled traffic to be switched between the Main and Windsor lines and into almost all of the platforms, giving considerable flexibility in working, especially in emergency. Often a down main line train leaving from old platforms Nos 12-14 would start out on the down Windsor local line as far as the West crossings, meanwhile an incoming train off the up main line could run into platforms Nos 7-11. Until Loco Junction box was abolished it was possible for down trains to cross from Windsor to Main lines there. Finally, at Queenstown Road Battersea there are double crossovers from Windsor to Main lines; some of the all-night trains to the Kingston Roundabout, which were steam-worked until the outbreak of war in 1939, have regularly used this connection. As part of the recent Waterloo resignalling a ladder crossover in the opposite direction between Windsor and Main fast lines has been provided at Nine Elms, at a location now beneath the flyover leading to the Chatham line. Occasionally, up Windsor line trains are diverted here to the Main line for stock transfer purposes, but construction work on the International station usually entailed closure of the Windsor lines between Waterloo and Clapham Junction.

World War 2 saw a drastic reduction in Waterloo's off-peak suburban services, but the SR tried to maintain adequate facilities for those commuters still at work in London. During the period of the 'blitz' the nightly interruptions by enemy action were so frequent that the starting point of the overnight mail and newspaper trains was transferred to Wimbledon or Surbiton. Though traffic to the South coast was reduced, trains to the West of England were packed with military and civilian travellers. During the last years of the war, 'Merchant Navy' Pacifics were hauling 16 coaches on the wartime version of the 'Atlantic Coast Express'. As the platforms at Waterloo were not long enough to handle such trains, incoming services had to be divided at Clapham Junction.

The return of peace brought a pent-up demand for holidays to a Southern Railway still short of rolling stock and motive power. On summer Saturdays vast crowds queuing for trains filled the concourse at Waterloo with many more in the streets outside waiting to enter the station. The introduction in 1947 of the 'Devon Belle' Pullman was a way of providing an extra train by using the cars which had been stored during the war. The non-stop 'Bournemouth Limited' was not restored, but in its place came the 'Royal Wessex', introduced in 1951 with new BR Mark 1 coaches. On a summer Saturday during the early 1950s 119 main line trains were scheduled to leave Waterloo. Excursion traffic also resumed; the Restalls and National Sunday League agency specials had ceased and the popular prewar visits to ocean liners at Southampton were much reduced, but Sunday mornings again saw a succession of well-filled trains leaving Waterloo for Portsmouth and Bournemouth. Ramblers' specials also enjoyed renewed popularity until four wheels replaced two legs and many of the most attractive destination stations were closed.

The overnight mail and newspaper trains had become known to servicemen during the war and had found their way into the public timetable. A BR leaflet quoted the 1.15am West Country newspaper train as the heaviest departure from Waterloo, its 450ton formation serving 95 stations. In 1958 it comprised 15 vehicles on Tuesdays to Fridays, with 17 on Mondays when weekend travellers were returning to home or barracks. The working notice specified that this train was to be brought in from Clapham Yard by a tank engine – tender locos often arrived at Waterloo with empty stock prior to taking out their own train, but the additional length would have found the leading vans off the end of platform No 11. Another long train was the Dorchester and Weymouth mail, then leaving Waterloo at 10.35pm. This arrived from Clapham in two sections, the passenger coaches and parcel vans into platform No 10 and the mail vans and TPO to load at platform 11, with the two parts being united in No 10 shortly before departure. The late fee post box on the concourse instructed correspondents where to find the TPO at the appropriate time. During the afternoon and early evening parcel trains stood loading in platforms Nos 12 and 15, so that Waterloo had less capacity for the homeward rush hour than for the morning peak arrivals.

The Portsmouth, Alton and Reading electrifications of the 1930s had simplified train working at Waterloo, but steam reigned supreme on the lines to Bournemouth and the West of England. Even in the 1950s every long distance train on arrival was taken back to Clapham Yard for servicing and a stud of Drummond 'M7' tanks was kept employed on this task. These were gradually replaced by ex-GWR pannier tanks and by 2-6-2Ts of LMS and BR design at the same time as the Southern 4-6-0 classes on main line duties gave way to BR Standard 4-6-0s and 2-6-0s.

Three 1Co-Co1 diesel locos, designed by the Southern Railway for the Exeter route, emerged in 1951-54 and joined by the two Co-Co diesels of LMS origin operated intermittently on four intensive diagrams between Waterloo, Exeter and Weymouth.

Following their transfer to the LMR, the growl of the diesel was not heard again at Waterloo until 1962, when some of the 1,550hp BRCW/Crompton Type 3 locos began to appear on boat trains and Saturday extras when steam heating was not required. The transfer of the lines west of Salisbury to the Western Region led to the introduction in September 1964 of a semi-fast service between Waterloo and Exeter worked by 'Warship' class diesel hydraulic locos, also to the end of the 'Atlantic Coast Express' and all its through coaches.

Electrification to Bournemouth had already been announced, with diesel traction beyond to Weymouth. During the transition period the remaining Bulleid Pacifics and Standard 4-6-0s were frequently relieved by diesels — Class 47s on some of the heavier steam-heated trains and the Cromptons (Class 33) on the unpowered TC sets intended to work with the REP electric tractor units as far as Bournemouth. During the first half of 1967 the platforms at Waterloo were lined with tape recorders, cameras and cines chronicling for posterity the last normal steam workings into a London terminus. Finally, on the evening of 9 July, No 35030 brought the ultimate steam train into Waterloo.

A complete new timetable followed the electrification and non-standard trains such as the 'Bournemouth Belle' disappeared. The name 'Royal Wessex' was dropped only to be revived in 1988 at the time of the Weymouth electrification, when the REP/TC formations were replaced by the new Class 442 'Wessex' EMUs. Boat trains to Southampton have virtually ceased; mail, newspaper and parcels trains are no more and in 1993 the Class 159 DMUs replaced loco haulage on the Exeter service.

Adams 'Jubilee' 0-4-2 No 556 stands at the end of platform No 2, waiting to take out a train for Guildford via Cobham. The roof and platforms of the South station can be seen behind the loco.
Ian Allan Library

Waterloo has now become a terminus given over to the simple in and out routine of multiple-unit operation. The scene has changed over the years; 4-CORs and 2-BILs have been succeeded by 4-CIGs (Class 421) and 4-VEPs (Class 423), while on the suburban lines there has been a progression from the SR's conversions of wooden-bodied steam stock through the slam door 4-SUB and EPB units to the sliding door designs of Classes 508 and 455. Saturdays, even in high summer, see only the standard pattern of departures and Sundays are a day of rest, with no excursions and only a limited service for much of the day. Ascot Races, once the sporting highlight of the year, requires only four additions to the normal half-hourly service.

The following table shows the pattern of scheduled departures from Waterloo over the years:

Train Services
Waterloo Departures – Mondays to Fridays

	1867	1890	1913	1922	1939	1960	1976	1992
Main Line								
Suburban	17	88	88	200	289	244	210	181
Outer Area	12	27	42	63	120	111	126	148
Long Distance	15	24	49	35	44	48	81	93
Total	44	139	179	298	453	403	417	422
Windsor Line								
Suburban	51	102	101	180	188	151	114	74
Outer Area	13	21	29	37	82	77	106	78
Total	64	123	130	217	270	228	220	152
All Departures	108	262	309	515	723	631	637	574

Notes:

Suburban: the routes to Epsom, Chessington, Hampton Court, Shepperton, Kingston Roundabout, East Putney, the Hounslow Loop and Kensington.

Outer Area: services to Guildford via Cobham and via Woking, Alton, Basingstoke (stopping trains), Chertsey, Windsor, Ascot and Reading.

Long Distance: Main line fast services to Portsmouth, Bournemouth and the West of England.

Departures comprise regular services advertised in the company or regional public timetable.

Another Adams design, the 'T1' 0-4-4Ts, was to be found on suburban traffic at the turn of the century. Here No 3 is being turned on the Windsor line table, while an Adams 'Radial' 4-4-2T stands in one of the platforms. Note the original cut-away shape of the North station roof.
Locomotive Publishing Co/IAL

The figures for Waterloo departures illustrate the growth of traffic during the LSWR and SR period, latterly encouraged by electrification, but they also show the drift of rail travellers away from the inner suburbs. Trains from Waterloo to Kensington ceased in 1912, those to Wimbledon via East Putney in 1941. On the electrified suburban routes postwar economies have cut services from Herbert Walker's 'every twenty minutes' to intervals of half an hour or more, while peak hour extras to places such as Hounslow or Strawberry Hill have been withdrawn. This has been offset by the increase in services to the outer areas following electrification to Portsmouth, Alton and Reading and more recently by the growth in main line traffic since the Bournemouth line was converted.

Train movements necessarily exceed the number of scheduled passenger trains, particularly in the days of parcel and milk trains, empty carriage workings and light engines. In 1906 the old station handled 652 trains on a normal weekday; following rebuilding and suburban electrification 1922 saw 1,159 movements daily. By 1939 this had reached 1,700 and after the wartime reduction it had recovered to 1,593 in 1954. The 1958 train service cuts reduced this figure, but the Bournemouth electrification swelled the figures again, which currently stand at 1,337 movements a day on Mondays to Fridays. In terms of passengers, 160,000 were using the station daily in 1939, with postwar traffic peaking at 223,000 in 1954 when commuters had to endure twice daily crush hours. Numbers fell to about 196,000 in the 1960s but recovered to a maximum of 210,000 in 1989, before dropping to 178,000 in 1992 as a result of the recession.

A busy scene in the new South station during the summer of 1910. Suburban trains formed of 'Bogie Block' sets are in platforms Nos 1 and 2, the latter bound for Teddington, while main line trains occupy platform Nos 3–5 — a departure for Bournemouth in No 3 and a Southampton arrival in No 4. Lens of Sutton

Far right, bottom: Seen from the 10.45am to Portsmouth, No 21C12 United States Lines stands at the head of the 10.50am 'Atlantic Coast Express' on 24 October 1946. Although not of the length of the 16-coach wartime train, No 21C12's footplate is far beyond the starting signal on platform No 10 so that the driver will have to be advised verbally when the green is displayed, but the loco may be so far forward that advance track circuits are occupied and the signal cannot be cleared; in which case the power box will have to authorise the start by hand signal or telephone message. G. J. Jefferson

Waterloo has been relatively fortunate in respect of accidents. The most serious took place at Vauxhall on 29 August 1912 when the driver of a light engine running from Nine Elms to Waterloo misread signals and collided with a train from Aldershot which was standing in the station while tickets were being collected. One passenger was killed and over 50 injured. The files of official accident inquiries contain many reports of minor collisions and derailments in and around Waterloo, some of them arising from the difficulty in working traffic during fog, so prevalent in smoky London. Most accidents caused more disruption than casualties, but a fatal collision on 5 May 1905 between an up Reading service and a milk train was a forerunner of the 1988 Clapham Junction disaster as it was due to a linesman's error.

Queen Victoria found Waterloo inconvenient and continued to use a private platform at Nine Elms until 1876. The two succeeding monarchs both preferred to depart from Victoria on their frequent journeys to Portsmouth, so it is only in fairly recent years that Waterloo has enjoyed much royal patronage. In 1939 and in 1947 the Royal Family departed from Waterloo on tours of America and South Africa respectively, while in 1923, 1947 and 1981 the terminus has been the starting point for royal honeymoons. Among other special occasions have been the State funerals of Sir Winston Churchill in 1965 and of Earl Mountbatten in 1979.

One benefit of the collapse of the property boom has been to remove the temptation for developers to build over the air space above the platforms. Waterloo has become one of London's most attractive stations, only rivalled by the rebuilt Liverpool Street, and happily the advent of the International terminal has done nothing to detract from it.

Right:
Two 4-4-0s 'T9' No 711 and 'L11' No 440 wait for the road at Vauxhall East box signals while en route from Nine Elms to Waterloo in 1919.
C. J. Housego

Below right:
'Lord Nelson' No 851 Sir Francis Drake *waits in platform No 7 with a down Bournemouth express in about 1932. The semaphore starting signals on each platform were arranged vertically — to local or through lines, for a shunt movement and at bottom the calling on arm.*
Alan A. Jackson collection.

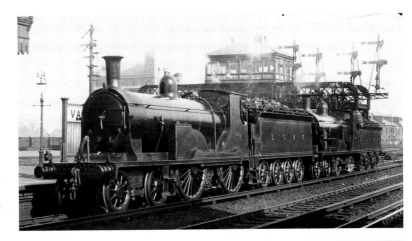

Right:
A glimpse of Nine Elms loco depot in the immediate post-Nationalisation period. 'West Country' Blackmore Vale, still in Southern livery, has received its BR number 34023, but Drummond 'Paddlebox' 4-6-0s Nos 447 and 444 still carry the SR's wartime black (the latter was never renumbered).
P. Ransome-Wallis

Centre right:
As part of British Railways' quest for a suitable livery, No 30864 Sir Martin Frobisher *in apple green and a train of new Bulleid coaches in 'plum and spilt milk' displayed themselves daily on the 3.30pm Waterloo-Bournemouth, seen here on 24 June 1948 crossing the bridge over Lambeth Road.* British Rail

Bottom right:
To brighten the postwar scene at Waterloo, the SR had repainted in malachite green some of the 'M7' tanks used on empty stock workings. In this picture of No 30244 British Railways' lettering had replaced the Southern title, but the green livery has been retained.
Locomotive Publishing Co/IAL

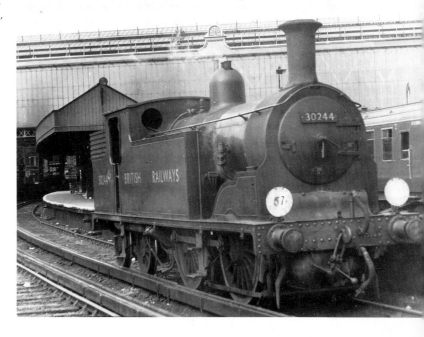

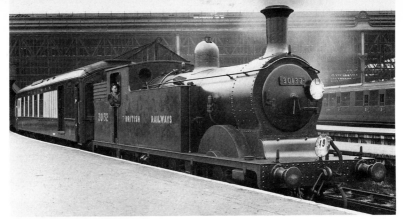

Right:
More usual livery for the 'M7s' was the wartime black, but No 30132 has had the 'British Railways' title added in the SR's style of 'sunshine' lettering, when seen in August 1948 about to leave Waterloo with the empty Pullmans of the 'Bournemouth Belle'.
R. F. Roberts

Centre right:
The RAF Display at Farnborough in July 1950 brought some unusual sights to Waterloo. A special seen passing Vauxhall on 7 July was headed by Brighton Atlantic No 32421 South Foreland *(which had been a regular visitor during the war years), but its train of Westinghouse-fitted GER compartment stock was something never seen before or (happily) since; an opinion shared by those spectators whose trains reached Farnborough after the show had started.*
Denis Cullum

Bottom right:
Two of the new Standard 'Britannia' Pacifics were allocated to Nine Elms in 1951 and were often used on the 'Bournemouth Belle' Here No 70009 Alfred the Great *enters Waterloo on 25 May 1951 with an Institution of Mechanical Engineers special from Southampton.*
Denis Cullum

Right:
The practice commenced in 1952 of naming the principal Southampton Docks boat trains. On 10 July light Pacific No 34018 Axminster *passes Vauxhall with the all-Pullman 11.54am from Waterloo, the first down 'Statesman' train run in connection with the liner* United States. *These important services usually ran to and from platform No 11.* Denis Cullum

Below:
During the summer of 1953 crank-axle flaws on the Bulleid Pacifics brought some unusual substitutes to Waterloo. Here on 14 May, Eastern Region 'V2' 2-6-2 No 60917 leaves on a gentle running-in turn on the 3.54pm to Basingstoke. Denis Cullum

Right:
Ex-LMS 'Black 5' 4-6-0s were also drafted in and here No 45061 stands at the head of the 1.24pm to Basingstoke on 6 June 1953. R. F. Roberts

Centre right:
The boat specials which ran on summer Saturdays in connection with ocean cruises did not share the prestigious motive power or stock of the named trains. On 11 July 1953 'H15' 4-6-0 No 30486 leaves platform No 13 with the 11.35am Orient Line special. Standing in platform No 12 is the 11.40am to Portsmouth Harbour, one of the fast trains leaving this platform every half hour with reserved seat passengers who queued in the central roadway to be admitted through the gates midway along the platform. Author

Bottom right:
Vauxhall could often provide an interesting variety of neck and neck views as two trains ran parallel on the Main and Windsor lines. In May 1957, No 35029 Ellerman Lines *on a down Bournemouth express and 'M7' tank No 30319 on a down empty stock train approach the station together.* Brian Morrison

Right:
Two years later, on 16 May 1959, the WR Pannier tanks had begun to replace the 'M7s' and here No 4692 is being overtaken by No 34048 Crediton *on the 2.30pm to Weymouth.*
Author

Below right:
Dieselisation of the Cross-London freight traffic made some of the 'W' class 2-6-4Ts available to replace Feltham's Urie 'H16' tanks on empty stock workings into Waterloo. On a typical summer day on 6 July 1963, No 31917 heads down the Windsor line towards Clapham Junction through Vauxhall with the empty milk tanks which had spent the morning in the up Windsor local platform there being unloaded.
Author

Below:
The final years of steam at Waterloo saw LMS and BR design tank engines on the empty carriage duties. During steam's last week, on 7 July 1967, Class 4 2-6-4T No 80015 approaches Vauxhall with the stock for the 18.30 to Weymouth. Author

Right:
As steam traction neared its end, all kinds of unusual locos visited Waterloo on rail tours. On 26 March 1966 'A4' Pacific No 60024 *Kingfisher backs down on to its train.*
M. R. Walkden

Below:
Brand new SR-designed 1Co-Co1 diesel-electric No 10202 passes Vauxhall on 25 September 1951 while running-in on the 11.54am to Salisbury. Its sister, No 10201, was not far away, being still on display on the Belvedere Road turntable within the Festival of Britain exhibition.
Denis Cullum

Above:
Class K Mogul No 32338 was not a diesel loco, but on 5 February 1953 it carried out clearance trials on the Windsor line side of Waterloo, apparently in connection with the further use of diesel traction. One of the SR-design locos can be seen in the North sidings, alongside tank wagons of diesel fuel.
Denis Cullum

Centre right:
The following month the two LMS-design diesels joined the three SR ones on South Western services. On the murky morning of 5 March 1953 No 10000 makes its first trip on the 8.30am to Weymouth.
Denis Cullum

Right:
After the last of the five prototype main line diesels had left the SR in 1955, several years elapsed before diesel traction reappeared at Waterloo. From the summer of 1962 the BRCW/Crompton locos (now Class 33) designed for SR use began to visit the terminus. No D6504 arrives on 6 July 1962 with the 7.03am Le Havre boat train from Southampton Docks. A. G. Dixon

Right:
The Class 33s became the mainstay of SR diesel operation and during the late 1970s were in charge of the Waterloo-Exeter service. In October 1979 No 33027 is seen leaving Waterloo for Exeter from the same viewpoint as 'T9' No 307 (seen earlier) was taken in 1902.
C. J. Marsden

Below:
When the WR revised the Waterloo West of England services in 1964, they introduced the 'Warship' type diesel-hydraulic locos. Through the old Bostick gates of platform No 14, No D870 Zulu is seen with an arrival from Exeter on 9 March 1971.
J. H. Cooper-Smith

Above:
Latterly the 'Warship'
diesels became increasingly
unreliable and on 23 July
1971, No 806 Cambrian
required assistance from
electro-diesel No E6015 on
the 13.08 to Exeter.
R. E. Ruffell

Right:
Successors to the
'Warships' and
'Cromptons' were the Class
50 diesels. Soon after their
introduction to the Exeter
service No 50035 Ark
Royal leaves with the 19.10
train on 24 May 1981.
Barry Edwards

Right:
The final years of loco haulage on the West of England line were the responsibility of the Class 47/7 series transferred from ScotRail to Network SouthEast. No 47705 stands in new platform No 13 with the 08.10 from Exeter on 11 March 1993.
Author

Centre right:
Diesel railcars have never been a prominent feature of the Waterloo scene. WR DMUs appeared occasionally during 1965/66, while the SR's DEMUs have mainly been seen deputising for loco-hauled services in emergency or on summer Saturdays. After the Clapham Junction-Kensington service was taken over by one of these units in May 1990, it returned westward on a late night departure from Waterloo. Hampshire unit No 1116 made the first trip to Waterloo on 1 November 1962 covering a steam roster on the 10.54am to Salisbury. J. Scrace

Bottom right:
The three SR-designed electric locos only visited Waterloo for trials or on special occasions. No 20002 is seen here passing Vauxhall on 2 May 1952 with a special to Portsmouth for a City livery company, formed of ex-LNER stock.
Denis Cullum

Above:
One of the short-lived Class 74 electro-diesels, No 74005, is in charge of the 09.36 Waterloo-Weymouth Quay Channel Islands boat train approaching Vauxhall on 21 June 1977.
B. Denton

Right:
The return working of the Weymouth boat train stands in platform No 11 on 6 October 1981 headed by one of the capable Class 73 electro-diesels No 73138.
C. J. Marsden

Below right:
A train of 4-COR units passes Vauxhall with a down Portsmouth semi-fast service in 1966. The photographer's vantage point is Coronation Buildings, one of the tenement blocks erected by the LSWR to accommodate families displaced by the widening of the line out of Waterloo during the early 1900s. The tall chimney on the right marks the dairy and bottling plant which was the objective of the milk trains to Vauxhall.
J. F. Bradshaw

Right:
The start of the 4-EPB era. New unit No 5001, having been inspected by Mr R. A. Riddles and other Railway Executive top brass, departs on a trial run to Guildford on 14 January 1952.
Denis Cullum

Below right:
A line-up of 4-SUB units in platforms Nos 1-6 during the evening rush hour on 9 June 1961. From left to right: the 5.54pm to Dorking, the 5.52pm to Guildford via Cobham, the 5.57pm to Chessington, the 6.00pm to Shepperton, the 5.52pm to Effingham Junction via Leatherhead and the 5.54pm to Hampton Court. Author

Below:
A contrast in 4-SUB front ends on 23 July 1971. No 4131 on the Kingston Roundabout (21) train was a hybrid unit incorporating HAL motor coaches, while No 4754 on the Effingham Junction (16) train is of standard design.
R. E. Ruffell

Above:
Two 4-SUB units arrive with an Effingham Junction train at platform No 4 on 3 October 1977. The complex track layout outside these platforms was shortly to be simplified. J. G. Glover

Right:
At the shortened platforms Nos 1-3 on 27 July 1980 stand three of the Class 508 units which spent about three years on the Waterloo suburban routes before moving to Merseyside, but leaving one of their trailer vehicles behind to be incorporated in the replacement Class 455 stock. R. E. Ruffell

Below right:
The changeover is in progress on 28 April 1984. 4-EPB No 5127 will work the 15.16 for the Kingston Roundabout, Class 455 unit No 5804 is on the 15.12 to Effingham Junction, while a Class 508 coach can be glimpsed in platform No 4.
C. J. Marsden

Right:
Two Class 442 units approach Vauxhall on 14 April 1988 with an inaugural special to celebrate the Weymouth electrification. The double crossover linking fast and slow lines had been added since the picture of No 74005 taken at the same location in 1977.
Brian Morrison

Below right:
The face of Waterloo in 1993. On 6 July, Class 442 'Wessex Electric' unit No 2422 departs from platform No 10 on the 10.32 'Channel Islands Express' for Weymouth, as Class 421/5 'Portsmouth Greyhound' 4-CIG unit No 1302 arrives with the 07.50 from Portsmouth Harbour. Meanwhile in platform No 12 Class 159 DMU No 159017 heads the 10.35 to Exeter St Davids.
Brian Morrison

Bottom right:
During the afternoon and evening platform No 15 housed the 8.13pm parcels train for the Reading line, but on a Sunday in April 1985 the platform was available for a special mail train to Southampton headed by No 73140.
C. J. Marsden

94

Right:
The small hours saw Waterloo busy with newspaper traffic until this was lost in 1988. Electro-diesel No 74009 stands at the head of the 02.15 newspaper special to Bournemouth on 7 October 1974. Brian Morrison

Below right:
The Bournemouth train was followed by the 02.30 to Portsmouth, diesel hauled by No 33021 on 7 October 1974. Were the 'Brute' trolleys in the background responsible for the crumbling edge of platform No 11? Brian Morrison

Below:
The 'Brighton Belle' units were often used for Royal journeys within the electrified network and could then be seen at Waterloo. On 20 July 1951 unit No 3052 forms a 'Deepdene' special to Portsmouth & Southsea for a member of the Royal family, seen here approaching Vauxhall. Denis Cullum

Right:
Royal trains on the SR were usually short Pullman or even EMU formations and it was probably unique to see the full ex-LNWR Royal train at Waterloo. This happened on 3 July 1952, when Her Majesty Queen Elizabeth II had carried out a tour in the West Country staying overnight in the train, which she had rejoined at Yeovil Junction for the return to Waterloo behind 'Merchant Navy' Pacific No 35025 Brocklebank Line, *seen here approaching Vauxhall.* Denis Cullum

Centre right:
The more usual style of Royal train was seen at Vauxhall on 2 August 1979 when HM the Queen Mother returned from Portsmouth Harbour. Electro-diesel No 73142 (not yet named Broadlands) *was hauling a composite four-car set of TC and REP stock.* C. J. Marsden

Bottom right:
Twice in recent years Waterloo has been the departure point from London for State funerals. On 30 January 1965 the special carrying the body of Sir Winston Churchill to Handborough is seen approaching Vauxhall on the down Windsor line. *Appropriately the loco is No 34051* Winston Churchill *and SR bogie luggage van No 2464 with the coffin has been painted in the colours of the accompanying Pullman cars.* Brian Coates

Select Bibliography

It has only been possible here to outline the history of Waterloo — the station, its trains and traffic, its motive power and rolling stock. The following books are suggested for further reading:

London's Termini (2nd edition), Alan A. Jackson, David & Charles 1985

History of the LSWR (Two Vols), R. A. Williams, David & Charles 1968 and 1973

The LSWR in the Twentieth Century, J. N. Faulkner & R. A. Williams, David & Charles 1988

History of the Southern Railway, C. Dendy Marshall revised R. W. Kidner, Ian Allan 1968

Sir Herbert Walker's Southern Railway, C. F. Klapper, Ian Allan 1973

Southern Electric (Fifth edition), G. T. Moody, Ian Allan 1979

South Eastern Railway, Adrian Gray, Middleton Press 1990

LSWR Locomotive History (Two Vols), D. L. Bradley, RCTS 1965 and 1967

Southern Railway Locomotive History (Two Vols), D. L. Bradley, RCTS 1975 and 1976

LSWR Carriages, G. R. Weddell, Wild Swan 1992

Maunsell's SR Steam Passenger Stock, D. Gould, Oakwood 1978

Bulleid's SR Steam Passenger Stock, D. Gould, Oakwood 1980